Ruth, Esther, Song of Songs

A Word Find Book *from* Our Daily Bread Ministries

Our Daily Bread
Publishing®

Ruth, Esther, Song of Songs: A Word Find Book from Our Daily Bread Ministries
Puzzles © 2025 by Christopher Hudson & Associates

All rights reserved.

"Quick Answers" and "Top Ten" text excerpted from *Our Daily Bread Bible Sourcebook* © 2019 Discovery House. Used by permission.

Requests for permission to quote from this book should be directed to: Permissions Department, Our Daily Bread Publishing, PO Box 3566, Grand Rapids, MI 49501; or contact us by email at permissionsdept@odbm.org.

Scripture quotations taken from the Holy Bible, New International Version®, NIV®. Copyright © 1973, 1978, 1984, 2011 by Biblica, Inc.™ Used by permission of Zondervan. All rights reserved worldwide. www.zondervan.com. The "NIV" and "New International Version" are trademarks registered in the United States Patent and Trademark Office by Biblica, Inc.™

The Search the Scriptures series has been created by Peachtree Publishing Services, a book project management company with a passion for and focus on Bible-related projects. With a full suite of editorial services, they manage complex projects for the world's leading Bible and Christian book publishers.

Interior design by Mike Williams

ISBN: 978-1-64070-378-0

Printed in the United States of America
25 26 27 28 29 30 31 32 / 8 7 6 5 4 3 2 1

Welcome to the Search the Scriptures series. This series was designed to bring your love of puzzles and the Bible together. From beginning to end, this book will engage readers of all ages—whether 8 or 88—with the transformational stories and teachings of the Bible.

This book offers a great way to unwind and meditate on teachings from Scripture while solving fun puzzles. Throughout, you'll find

- the full NIV Bible text of Ruth, Esther, and Song of Songs alongside word search puzzles;
- articles at the beginning of each book that offer deeper insights; and
- bonus puzzles and crosswords that highlight key words and themes.

Each Scripture-based word search or crossword provides clues that require you to look in the text for the answer before finding the word in the puzzle. You'll reinforce your knowledge of the Bible or encounter it for the first time in a fun, interactive way. And if you ever need help, there's an answer key in the back—but don't peek too soon!

We hope you'll have fun as you're also drawn deeper into the power of God's Word. Enjoy the journey!

—The Editors

RUTH

Quick Answers

The words you need to solve this puzzle are highlighted in bold below.

WHO

Who Wrote It?

Tradition gives the nod to **Samuel** for the little book.

Who's in It?

Elimelek, Ruth, Naomi, **Orpah**, Boaz

WHAT

Who doesn't like this story? It has **drama** (a family must move across the river in order to get food). It has **tragedy** (Naomi loses her husband and her sons to death). We don't know the details about these three deaths—perhaps they occur in battle, perhaps they are due to disease, or maybe they are the results of an accident. But we can only imagine the **heartbreak** and **sadness** that must accompany these three women. **Naomi** and Ruth have no means of **support** as they arrive in Bethlehem, and they must depend on the **kindness** of others. But God has gone before to set things up for them, and the surprising outcome becomes a flashpoint of **joy** in the midst of a dark time in Israel's history.

WHEN

Naomi and her family had stayed for ten years in **Moab**, and we don't know how long they stayed in Bethlehem on their return. We do know that this event took place during the time of the **Judges**, which was between 1350 and 1050 BC.

WHERE

As noted above, the story starts in **Bethlehem**, moves to Moab, and concludes back in Bethlehem.

WHY

Naomi and her husband Elimelek have migrated out of the Promised Land, moving from Bethlehem to Moab because of a **food shortage**. In Moab, they do not find life easy. Naomi loses three family members: her husband and her two sons. There is no peace in Moab. Yet on her return to Israel with her widowed daughter-in-law, she finds **peace**. And Ruth finds Boaz. It's a picture of the comfort found in trusting God and staying in fellowship and unity with Him.

```
V Q F T O A G F J Z U U B Q E
X M Y R M H O O E H K H F W N
K H P A H M T O B G R G Y J Z
X A R G W S P D U M T X E Q K
H D R E V N L S S E N D A S E
K F O D R X J H J B A O M K L
U B Q Y O Q V O C K G G W C E
I J G Y H E A R T B R E A K M
X Y A H M B C T N T P B G R I
E O G M P J L A S R I B C L L
P T K L V H D G K O U P L G E
C Y E E A E T E W P E K A B J
Q V W U O O U Y M P H R E I S
G C O M W T O S J U F T P H S
U L W A B Y G Q K S H I G I E
P V J S O E O H V L R P H M N
E P W L O Q R J E Y S C G O D
A L U G K J I H V K J C H A N
C X S W G Z E I A W R H D N I
E Y E X Y M D J U D G E S A K
```

Answer key on page 83

7

Top 10 Key Facts about the Book of Ruth

The words you need to solve this puzzle are highlighted in bold below.

1. Ruth would become the great grandmother of Israel's **King David**.
2. Moabites were noted as being a pagan people, yet this story reveals that a **Moabite** woman was **grafted** into the **family line** of **Jesus** himself.
3. The term "**guardian-redeemer**" appears nine times in the New International Version of the book of Ruth. This was a **relative** who had means and who could be depended upon by other family members in a time of need.
4. Ruth pictures for us what **redemption** looks like. She rejected her old pagan way and stood strong for her faith by forsaking the old and openly accepting God's love for her and giving Him control over her life. She shined in an era of darkness (the Judges era).
5. The name of **Boaz**, who can be seen as a type of Christ, meant "**strength**."
6. Contrasting with the horrific final chapters of Judges, this benign, **peaceful** love story that follows provides the reader with **hope** and joy before heading into the complicated stories of Hebrew monarchies.
7. In the Hebrew version of the Old Testament, this book appears after the book of Proverbs. You will notice that Ruth is referred to as a "woman of **noble character**" (3:11), an appellation that is repeated in Proverbs 31.
8. The **chivalrous** behavior of Boaz toward Ruth as she visited him in the night is a model for all men as they consider how to treat women (Ruth 3:1–9).
9. Take note that the setting for this all-important story in Israel's history is **Bethlehem**, which plays an integral part in God's story.
10. Ruth's story is a picture of God's **grace**. According to Deuteronomy 23:3, "no . . . Moabite . . . may enter the assembly of the Lord." God's grace overrides the law—especially when God's plan is in view.

```
Y H A C A M Y V T C J U Z E T
E N I L Y L I M A F I H L U M
B B R K Q D V N R L L O A Q U
E S I R E I L K T Y U B X F R
P U U Y Q K T I S Q F S F E E
R S T I J M O B U M E S G S M
K E H Q J A N K O Y C J F J E
I J T H V Y T A R L A Z Z R E
N I G C J I B U L I E N Y E D
G L N D A I D D A E P O H D E
D A E M T R S E V I T A L E R
A L R E P C A W I G M H K M N
V T T L E X J H H J F J M P A
I I S R B E K J C W M O S T I
D Y Z M F W K U E G L O I D
Z A G Y C E P X K Z L Z E O R
D E T F A R G H I J B B P N A
G K B E T H L E H E M O O F U
Q F J I C N V P U H X V A N G
A U V E C A R G X P P Z W Z D
```

Answer key on page 83

9

Ruth

Naomi Loses Her Husband and Sons

1 In the days when the judges ruled, there was a famine in the land. So a man from Bethlehem in Judah, together with his wife and two sons, went to live for a while in the country of Moab. ²The man's name was Elimelek, his wife's name was Naomi, and the names of his two sons were Mahlon and Kilion. They were Ephrathites from Bethlehem, Judah. And they went to Moab and lived there.

³Now Elimelek, Naomi's husband, died, and she was left with her two sons. ⁴They married Moabite women, one named Orpah and the other Ruth. After they had lived there about ten years, ⁵both Mahlon and Kilion also died, and Naomi was left without her two sons and her husband.

Naomi and Ruth Return to Bethlehem

⁶When Naomi heard in Moab that the Lord had come to the aid of his people by providing food for them, she and her daughters-in-law prepared to return home from there. ⁷With her two daughters-in-law she left the place where she had been living and set out on the road that would take them back to the land of Judah.

⁸Then Naomi said to her two daughters-in-law, "Go back, each of you, to your mother's home. May the Lord show you kindness, as you have shown kindness to your dead husbands and to me. ⁹May the Lord grant that each of you will find rest in the home of another husband."

Then she kissed them goodbye and they wept aloud ¹⁰and said to her, "We will go back with you to your people."

¹¹But Naomi said, "Return home, my daughters. Why would you come with me? Am I going to have any more sons, who could become your husbands? ¹²Return home, my daughters; I am too old to have another husband. Even if I thought there was still hope for me — even if I had a husband tonight and then gave birth to sons — ¹³would you wait until they grew up? Would you remain unmarried for them? No, my daughters. It is more bitter for me than for you, because the Lord's hand has turned against me!"

¹⁴At this they wept aloud again. Then Orpah kissed her mother-in-law goodbye, but Ruth clung to her.

¹⁵"Look," said Naomi, "your sister-in-law is going back to her people and her gods. Go back with her."

"Naomi" means "pleasant," whereas "Mara" means "bitter."

```
O K G Z G S G N N Y P G V I G N O H P
P R X O S S E N D N I K M I B Q Z E G
M Q B Q D X W T F W B O K B J T O A S
K R R W P S R X M A A I R A N P V W U
T O W E C L U N G N D D K A L J Z E R
C A D D T J T S O V K D N E Q Z Y P Y
Y H D G A U H U S B A N D K X A L T O
B O I V W N R E L I M E L E K T Y J T
F G R H D Z E N E A E E Q K Q B U I T
T M I D E S S I K H L D R I K D H F Q
N D K T G W I L G S H W A U G T A W V
B F W K S D P D N E A B C E N M P Q B
B E T H L E H E M T D Y S H I Z R A S
X Y W J M P K Q U P U L W N V T O C W
G Z R E T T I B C J J U E W U M B P A
```

1. This story takes place in the days when the <u>J</u> <u>U</u> <u>D</u> <u>G</u> <u>E</u> <u>S</u> ruled. (1:1)
2. In those days, there was a _ _ _ _ _ _ _ in the land. (1:1)
3. A family from Judah went to live in the country of _ _ _ _ _. (1:1)
4. The man's name was _ _ _ _ _ _ _ _ _. (1:2)
5. His wife's name was _ _ _ _ _ _. (1:2)
6. They were Ephrathites from _ _ _ _ _ _ _ _ _. (1:2)
7. After Naomi's _ _ _ _ _ _ _ died, her two sons married Moabite women. (1:3)
8. One of these Moabite women was named _ _ _ _ _. (1:4)
9. The other Moabite woman was named _ _ _ _ _. (1:4)
10. Naomi heard that the Lord had come to the aid of his _ _ _ _ _ _ _. (1:6)
11. Naomi set out on the road that would take them back to _ _ _ _ _ _. (1:7)
12. Naomi hoped the Lord would show _ _ _ _ _ _ _ _ _ to her daughters-in-law. (1:8)
13. Naomi's daughters-in-law _ _ _ _ _ aloud. (1:9)
14. Naomi said to them, "_ _ _ _ _ _ _ home, my daughters." (1:11)
15. Naomi said it was more _ _ _ _ _ _ _ for her than for them. (1:13)
16. Orpah _ _ _ _ _ _ _ her mother-in-law goodbye. (1:14)
17. Ruth _ _ _ _ _ _ to Naomi. (1:14)
18. Naomi said, "Your sister-in-law is going back to her people and her _ _ _ _ _." (1:15)

Answer key on page 83

¹⁶But Ruth replied, "Don't urge me to leave you or to turn back from you. Where you go I will go, and where you stay I will stay. Your people will be my people and your God my God. ¹⁷Where you die I will die, and there I will be buried. May the LORD deal with me, be it ever so severely, if even death separates you and me." ¹⁸When Naomi realized that Ruth was determined to go with her, she stopped urging her.

¹⁹So the two women went on until they came to Bethlehem. When they arrived in Bethlehem, the whole town was stirred because of them, and the women exclaimed, "Can this be Naomi?"

²⁰"Don't call me Naomi," she told them. "Call me Mara, because the Almighty has made my life very bitter. ²¹I went away full, but the LORD has brought me back empty. Why call me Naomi? The LORD has afflicted me; the Almighty has brought misfortune upon me."

²²So Naomi returned from Moab accompanied by Ruth the Moabite, her daughter-in-law, arriving in Bethlehem as the barley harvest was beginning.

Ruth Meets Boaz in the Grain Field

2 Now Naomi had a relative on her husband's side, a man of standing from the clan of Elimelek, whose name was Boaz.

²And Ruth the Moabite said to Naomi, "Let me go to the fields and pick up the leftover grain behind anyone in whose eyes I find favor."

Naomi said to her, "Go ahead, my daughter." ³So she went out, entered a field and began to glean behind the harvesters. As it turned out, she was working in a field belonging to Boaz, who was from the clan of Elimelek.

⁴Just then Boaz arrived from Bethlehem and greeted the harvesters, "The LORD be with you!"

"The LORD bless you!" they answered.

⁵Boaz asked the overseer of his harvesters, "Who does that young woman belong to?"

⁶The overseer replied, "She is the Moabite who came back from Moab with Naomi. ⁷She said, 'Please let me glean and gather among the sheaves behind the harvesters.' She came into the field and has remained here from morning till now, except for a short rest in the shelter."

⁸So Boaz said to Ruth, "My daughter, listen to me. Don't go and glean in another field and don't go away from here. Stay here with the women who work for me. ⁹Watch the field where the men are harvesting, and follow along after the women. I have told the men not to lay a hand on you. And whenever you are thirsty, go and get a drink from the water jars the men have filled."

¹⁰At this, she bowed down with her face to the ground. She asked him, "Why have I found such favor in your eyes that you notice me — a foreigner?"

The practice of gleaning was protected by Mosaic Law so that there would be grain left for the poor and for foreigners.

```
E V G F I E L D K D J S K G J T E V M
Y Y T P M E R F D A G H M F N R U I O
E J G D P Q M X G D I E H T T O N V Y
L K G E Q W R B O O M A E Y Z R W R Q
R P A N Z S A V F S Q V U Z W H Z B Z
A U E I Z C D T D W P E U S J A O M B
B J V M N Q E Q E A E S G S O D W G E
T M I R M I B Y U R O D W B Z N C V T
A A T E L F Z P S A P I E L G J N W H
V Z A T C J D Y C M L L K T M A U C L
U L L E Y I B X L G E R Z X E O X R E
V K E D O J L D F P X F N L U W V N H
B S R E T S E V R A H Y G I D Y G T E
I O J V B A S W I A C V Z P X L V O M
V F A V O R S Y A T S W M W G E A E D
```

1. Ruth said, "Where you go I will go, and where you ___ ___ ___ I will stay." (1:16)
2. Ruth declared, "Your _____ will be my people." (1:16)
3. Ruth promised, "Your ___ ___ ___ will be my God." (1:16)
4. Ruth said, "Where you ___ ___ ___ I will die." (1:17)
5. Naomi realized Ruth was _____ to go with her. (1:18)
6. When they arrived in _____, the town was stirred. (1:19)
7. Naomi asked to be called ___ ___ ___ ___, because her life was bitter. (1:20)
8. Naomi says she went away full, but the Lord brought her back ___ ___ ___ ___ ___. (1:21)
9. Naomi and Ruth arrived as the _____ harvest was beginning. (1:22)
10. Naomi had a _____ on her husband's side. (2:1)
11. The man's name was ___ ___ ___ ___. (2:1)
12. Ruth began to ___ ___ ___ ___ ___ in the fields belonging to Boaz. (2:3)
13. Boaz greeted the _____, "The LORD be with you!" (2:4)
14. They answered, "The LORD ___ ___ ___ ___ ___ ___ you!" (2:4)
15. Ruth had asked to glean and gather among the _____. (2:7)
16. Boaz told Ruth not to go and glean in another ___ ___ ___ ___ ___. (2:8)
17. Boaz told Ruth to drink from the ___ ___ ___ ___ ___ jars. (2:9)
18. Ruth asked why she had found such ___ ___ ___ ___ ___ in Boaz's eyes. (2:10)

Answer key on page 83

¹¹Boaz replied, "I've been told all about what you have done for your mother-in-law since the death of your husband — how you left your father and mother and your homeland and came to live with a people you did not know before. ¹²May the LORD repay you for what you have done. May you be richly rewarded by the LORD, the God of Israel, under whose wings you have come to take refuge."

¹³"May I continue to find favor in your eyes, my lord," she said. "You have put me at ease by speaking kindly to your servant — though I do not have the standing of one of your servants."

¹⁴At mealtime Boaz said to her, "Come over here. Have some bread and dip it in the wine vinegar."

When she sat down with the harvesters, he offered her some roasted grain. She ate all she wanted and had some left over. ¹⁵As she got up to glean, Boaz gave orders to his men, "Let her gather among the sheaves and don't reprimand her. ¹⁶Even pull out some stalks for her from the bundles and leave them for her to pick up, and don't rebuke her."

¹⁷So Ruth gleaned in the field until evening. Then she threshed the barley she had gathered, and it amounted to about an ephah. ¹⁸She carried it back to town, and her mother-in-law saw how much she had gathered. Ruth also brought out and gave her what she had left over after she had eaten enough.

¹⁹Her mother-in-law asked her, "Where did you glean today? Where did you work? Blessed be the man who took notice of you!"

Then Ruth told her mother-in-law about the one at whose place she had been working. "The name of the man I worked with today is Boaz," she said.

²⁰"The LORD bless him!" Naomi said to her daughter-in-law. "He has not stopped showing his kindness to the living and the dead." She added, "That man is our close relative; he is one of our guardian-redeemers."

²¹Then Ruth the Moabite said, "He even said to me, 'Stay with my workers until they finish harvesting all my grain.'"

²²Naomi said to Ruth her daughter-in-law, "It will be good for you, my daughter, to go with the women who work for him, because in someone else's field you might be harmed."

²³So Ruth stayed close to the women of Boaz to glean until the barley and wheat harvests were finished. And she lived with her mother-in-law.

Ruth and Boaz at the Threshing Floor

3 One day Ruth's mother-in-law Naomi said to her, "My daughter, I must find a home for you, where you will be well provided for. ²Now Boaz, with whose women you have worked, is a relative of ours. Tonight he will be winnowing barley on the threshing floor. ³Wash, put on perfume, and get dressed in your best clothes. Then go down to the threshing floor, but don't let him know you are there until he has finished eating and drinking. ⁴When he lies down, note the place where he is lying. Then go and uncover his feet and lie down. He will tell you what to do."

⁵"I will do whatever you say," Ruth answered. ⁶So she went down to the threshing floor and did everything her mother-in-law told her to do.

An ephah of barley would have weighed about thirty pounds.

```
I B T R Q R L P E V E N F D Q G E Z S
W H Y I P M K D C Q K A H J M O B T I
S O N A Z Z W M F Q B D J O V H G Z U
E W M H P T E I Y F G G U A R D I A N
L U P E E E W I N N O W I N G N N Q Z
D T T E N D R I V G P D U L F P H H M
N L F W H F E I D A S J A B P O A L B
U R B P E B T H R E S H I N G D H X L
B R A E R O T Z S E M G R A I N P O K
A H O M E L A N D E N Q L L B R E A D
S D X U Z K E O J W R Q F L X D K Y N
V I F F U I H X O O D H E W A O T T V
Q V N R C P W S G N I H T Y R E V E Z
P U Z E H R E J H W Q D N B S G Q C S
O H W P X A D E D I V O R P U X G R L
```

1. Boaz heard how Ruth had left her _ _ _ _ _ _ _ _ _ to live with a new people. (2:11)
2. He said, "May the Lord _ _ _ _ _ you for what you have done." (2:12)
3. He said that Ruth had taken refuge under the Lord's _ _ _ _ _ _. (2:12)
4. Boaz gave her _ _ _ _ _ with wine vinegar. (2:14)
5. He offered her roasted _ _ _ _ _ _. (2:14)
6. He told his men to leave some stalks from the _ _ _ _ _ _ _ _ for her. (2:16)
7. Ruth _ _ _ _ _ _ _ _ _ the barley she had gathered. (2:17)
8. Ruth's gleanings amounted to about an _ _ _ _ _. (2:17)
9. Naomi called Boaz a _ _ _ _ _ _ _ _ _-redeemer. (2:20)
10. Ruth stayed close to the _ _ _ _ _ _ of Boaz. (2:23)
11. Ruth gleaned until the barley and _ _ _ _ _ harvests were finished. (2:23)
12. Naomi wanted to find a home for Ruth, where she would be well _ _ _ _ _ _ _ _ _ for. (3:1)
13. She told Ruth that Boaz would be _ _ _ _ _ _ _ _ _ _ barley on the threshing floor. (3:2)
14. Naomi told Ruth to wash and put on _ _ _ _ _ _ _. (3:3)
15. Ruth was to go down to the _ _ _ _ _ _ _ _ _ floor. (3:3)
16. She was to uncover Boaz's _ _ _ _ _ and lie down. (3:4)
17. Ruth did _ _ _ _ _ _ _ _ _ _ her mother-in-law told her. (3:6)

Answer key on page 84

⁷When Boaz had finished eating and drinking and was in good spirits, he went over to lie down at the far end of the grain pile. Ruth approached quietly, uncovered his feet and lay down. ⁸In the middle of the night something startled the man; he turned — and there was a woman lying at his feet!

⁹"Who are you?" he asked.

"I am your servant Ruth," she said. "Spread the corner of your garment over me, since you are a guardian-redeemer of our family."

¹⁰"The LORD bless you, my daughter," he replied. "This kindness is greater than that which you showed earlier: You have not run after the younger men, whether rich or poor. ¹¹And now, my daughter, don't be afraid. I will do for you all you ask. All the people of my town know that you are a woman of noble character. ¹²Although it is true that I am a guardian-redeemer of our family, there is another who is more closely related than I. ¹³Stay here for the night, and in the morning if he wants to do his duty as your guardian-redeemer, good; let him redeem you. But if he is not willing, as surely as the LORD lives I will do it. Lie here until morning."

¹⁴So she lay at his feet until morning, but got up before anyone could be recognized; and he said, "No one must know that a woman came to the threshing floor."

¹⁵He also said, "Bring me the shawl you are wearing and hold it out." When she did so, he poured into it six measures of barley and placed the bundle on her. Then he went back to town.

¹⁶When Ruth came to her mother-in-law, Naomi asked, "How did it go, my daughter?"

Then she told her everything Boaz had done for her ¹⁷and added, "He gave me these six measures of barley, saying, 'Don't go back to your mother-in-law empty-handed.'"

¹⁸Then Naomi said, "Wait, my daughter, until you find out what happens. For the man will not rest until the matter is settled today."

Boaz Marries Ruth

4 Meanwhile Boaz went up to the town gate and sat down there just as the guardian-redeemer he had mentioned came along. Boaz said, "Come over here, my friend, and sit down." So he went over and sat down.

²Boaz took ten of the elders of the town and said, "Sit here," and they did so. ³Then he said to the guardian-redeemer, "Naomi, who has come back from Moab, is selling the piece of land that belonged to our relative Elimelek. ⁴I thought I should bring the matter to your attention and suggest that you buy it in the presence of these seated here and in the presence of the elders of my people. If you will redeem it, do so. But if you will not, tell me, so I will know. For no one has the right to do it except you, and I am next in line."

"I will redeem it," he said.

⁵Then Boaz said, "On the day you buy the land from Naomi, you also acquire Ruth the Moabite, the dead man's widow, in order to maintain the name of the dead with his property."

Winnowing uses the wind to remove chaff from grain.

```
G Q Y K C L S D X D W Q E P I E C E V
X T A S X R H V V R E Q V Q X T A G J
P N O B L E T R U Z H L C M Y P K O R
J F E E C E N T C T L T T I P G P R I
V N A X B C H H L T E Y I R A W H S G
Z N G Y L F M V X F J H O N A H D F H
F G F E E T O Y E L R A B I I T Z U T
S S S A K I N M U O C I S G O B S J M
A G F M X C B W G H Q R Z H N L T U E
D W U X Y W V Z E E N K S T E N N J E
P Z E L I P V D M N B F R R E T P O D
P W X F A S F D C F C X Q M E P J D E
D B C G J H H R O R Q E R L H D M B R
H P Q Q G F T I A W N A D G G C L V J
N T E L I M E L E K G X H Z G A T E F
```

1. Boaz lay down at the far end of the grain _ _ _ _. (3:7)
2. Ruth _ _ _ _ _ _ _ _ _ _ _ quietly and uncovered his feet. (3:7)
3. Something _ _ _ _ _ _ _ _ _ Boaz in the middle of the night. (3:8)
4. Ruth asked Boaz to spread the corner of his _ _ _ _ _ _ _ _ over her. (3:9)
5. Boaz called Ruth a woman of _ _ _ _ _ _ character. (3:11)
6. Boaz told Ruth to stay there for the _ _ _ _ _ _. (3:13)
7. Ruth lay at Boaz's _ _ _ _ until morning. (3:14)
8. Boaz gave Ruth six measures of _ _ _ _ _ _ _. (3:15)
9. Naomi told Ruth to _ _ _ _ _ until she found out what happened. (3:18)
10. Boaz sat down at the town _ _ _ _. (4:1)
11. Boaz called ten _ _ _ _ _ _ _ of the town to witness. (4:2)
12. He told them that Naomi was selling a _ _ _ _ _ _ of land. (4:3)
13. The land had belonged to _ _ _ _ _ _ _ _ _. (4:3)
14. The guardian-redeemer had the _ _ _ _ _ _ to redeem the land. (4:4)
15. The guardian-redeemer said, "I will _ _ _ _ _ _ _ it." (4:4)
16. Boaz then told him that acquiring the land meant acquiring _ _ _ _ _ the Moabite. (4:5)

⁶At this, the guardian-redeemer said, "Then I cannot redeem it because I might endanger my own estate. You redeem it yourself. I cannot do it."

⁷(Now in earlier times in Israel, for the redemption and transfer of property to become final, one party took off his sandal and gave it to the other. This was the method of legalizing transactions in Israel.)

⁸So the guardian-redeemer said to Boaz, "Buy it yourself." And he removed his sandal.

⁹Then Boaz announced to the elders and all the people, "Today you are witnesses that I have bought from Naomi all the property of Elimelek, Kilion and Mahlon. ¹⁰I have also acquired Ruth the Moabite, Mahlon's widow, as my wife, in order to maintain the name of the dead with his property, so that his name will not disappear from among his family or from his hometown. Today you are witnesses!"

¹¹Then the elders and all the people at the gate said, "We are witnesses. May the LORD make the woman who is coming into your home like Rachel and Leah, who together built up the family of Israel. May you have standing in Ephrathah and be famous in Bethlehem. ¹²Through the offspring the LORD gives you by this young woman, may your family be like that of Perez, whom Tamar bore to Judah."

Naomi Gains a Son

¹³So Boaz took Ruth and she became his wife. When he made love to her, the LORD enabled her to conceive, and she gave birth to a son. ¹⁴The women said to Naomi: "Praise be to the LORD, who this day has not left you without a guardian-redeemer. May he become famous throughout Israel! ¹⁵He will renew your life and sustain you in your old age. For your daughter-in-law, who loves you and who is better to you than seven sons, has given him birth."

¹⁶Then Naomi took the child in her arms and cared for him. ¹⁷The women living there said, "Naomi has a son!" And they named him Obed. He was the father of Jesse, the father of David.

The Genealogy of David

¹⁸This, then, is the family line of Perez:

Perez was the father of Hezron,
¹⁹Hezron the father of Ram,
Ram the father of Amminadab,
²⁰Amminadab the father of Nahshon,
Nahshon the father of Salmon,
²¹Salmon the father of Boaz,
Boaz the father of Obed,
²²Obed the father of Jesse,
and Jesse the father of David.

Rachel and Leah were the matriarchs of the twelve tribes of Israel.

```
H W H A E L R Z W K G N M C O O G V T
J I C Z I C O N C E I V E B Z S B W A
E T T C Z N D Y Z H Z Q O C W Q P L X
V N P H W O A F B V J D K A T D O V D
B E F I W A N M P R S H L Q S U I N
S S L E U V P E E C C P A V W A L R B
P S O O T X G C G A N X E N H W J F L
V E R X R N M O A B I T E C D N U Q I
K S D I A X F X E Z L A M E D A V I D
S X Q D E R D G Y N M G S S T L F H
I R N D D O T G R Z G D U N H S I H A
B E E L L J K A W G J E A K N R E F G
D L I D J H S J B G S B N L L E F J G
V H Z R L O P F F A M O U S U K G E M
C Q K L N E Z H A Z U M Q H Y A H W Y
```

1. The guardian-redeemer said redeeming the land might _ _ _ _ _ _ _ _ _ his own estate. (4:6)
2. He removed his _ _ _ _ _ _ _ as part of the legal transaction. (4:8)
3. Boaz announced to the _ _ _ _ _ _ _ and all the people that he would buy Naomi's property. (4:9)
4. Along with the property, Boaz acquired Ruth the _ _ _ _ _ _ _ _. (4:10)
5. Marrying Ruth allowed them to maintain the _ _ _ _ of the dead with his property. (4:10)
6. The people at the gate said, "We are _ _ _ _ _ _ _ _ _." (4:11)
7. The people blessed them, that Ruth may be like Rachel and _ _ _ _. (4:11)
8. They said, "May you be _ _ _ _ _ _ _ in Bethlehem." (4:11)
9. Boaz took Ruth and she became his _ _ _ _. (4:13)
10. The Lord enabled Ruth to _ _ _ _ _ _ _ _. (4:13)
11. She gave birth to a _ _ _. (4:13)
12. The women said to Naomi, "Praise be to the _ _ _ _." (4:14)
13. Naomi took the _ _ _ _ _ in her arms. (4:16)
14. They named the child _ _ _ _. (4:17)
15. Obed was the father of _ _ _ _ _ _. (4:22)
16. Obed's son was the father of _ _ _ _ _ _. (4:22)

Answer key on page 84

Highlights of Ruth

The next word search covers the full book of Ruth, highlighting some key words and themes from throughout the book.

- BARLEY
- BETHLEHEM
- BITTER
- BOAZ
- DAUGHTER IN LAW
- DAVID
- ELDERS
- ELIMELEK
- EPHAH
- FAMINE
- FAVOR
- FIELD
- FOREIGNER
- GLEAN
- GUARDIAN REDEEMER
- HARVEST
- ISRAEL
- JESSE
- JUDAH
- KINDNESS
- MOAB
- NAOMI
- OBED
- ORPAH
- PEREZ
- PROPERTY
- RUTH
- SANDAL
- SHEAVES
- THRESHING FLOOR

```
O G B O F D G S K H J Q S H Z T U Q F
W S A T D A U G H T E R I N L A W Q B
R E H T O D A E N L Q T E I F N O J Q
G R R S V J W J L S U Y Z P O R A M V
P U C E F O R E I G N E R X H T U J W
R B A V D I V A D K I L O P W A X T F
O Y R R N A X P T C C R R R F R H T H
P J L A D L M S O A F A X E O X W G W
E R E H W I B E M O A B P T Y E Z W
R T R S U B A G U W T K N L A D N A S
T E E C S B U N U K E K S A U I Q X M
Y I T W Z E I Q R L X S O R O Z Z J S
X Y T I A T S P O E E T G E E M A U K
O P I V L H R X J U D A H F R D I G E
S B B Q Z L A P L K F E N Z E F L L L
K V E C V E E I G F O Y E Y S K A E E
F F F D G H L P I I T R V M S A V A M
A S T R E E E S I T E N O W E A J N I
M B O A Z M L G P P Y C S L N R E R L
I V H H G Y I F I E L D U Q D H I V E
N Y B V Z B K I B E V P P M N A F Q V
E R F R R U C C T P X A N C I P A D R
R O O L F G N I H S E R H T K R V A V
X L J Q Z S A Y U O V E H H H O O Q Y
X S E V A E H S L L U M E K W P R S J
```

Answer key on page 84

Ruth

ACROSS

2. Future generations. (4:12)
5. Mother of Mahlon and Kilion. (1:2)
6. Home country of Ruth and Orpah. (1:1)
7. Famous king descended from Ruth. (4:17)
8. Time of day when Ruth spoke to Boaz at the threshing floor. (3:8)
11. Naomi's daughter-in-law. (1:4)
12. Name given to Ruth's child. (4:17)
13. Biblical woman compared to Ruth. (4:11)
14. Man of standing from Elimelek's clan. (2:1)
16. Boaz ensured Ruth did not go home in this way. (3:17)
17. Biblical woman compared to Ruth. (4:11)
20. Where Boaz waited to find the other relative. (4:1)
22. Come home after being away. (1:6)
23. Grandson of Ruth and Boaz. (4:17)
25. Ruth's mindset about staying with Naomi. (1:18)
27. Natural disaster that drove family into Moab. (1:1)
29. Where Boaz winnowed barley. (3:2)
33. Woman whose husband has died. (4:5)
35. Hometown of Naomi and Elimelek. (1:1)
36. The others gathering grain in Boaz's fields. (2:21)
37. Event that restored Naomi's joy. (4:13)

DOWN

1. Quality the Lord shows Naomi and Ruth through Boaz. (2:20)
3. Ruth's reputation. (3:11)
4. Meaning of "Mara." (1:20)
9. Boaz's family position toward Naomi and Ruth. (2:20)
10. Ruth's feeling toward Naomi. (4:15)
11. Safety found under the Lord's wings. (2:12)
15. Grain Ruth gathered. (2:17)
17. Property being sold by Naomi. (4:3)
18. A stranger in the land. (2:10)
19. Role of the elders and all the people. (4:9)
21. Time for collecting barley. (1:22)
24. Item given to redeem or transfer property. (4:7)
26. Pick up leftover grain in fields. (2:3)
27. What Ruth found in Boaz's eyes. (2:10)
28. Child born to Ruth and Boaz. (4:13)
30. What Naomi hoped to find for Ruth in Boaz. (3:1)
31. Ten townspeople who served as witnesses. (4:2)
32. What Ruth left behind to follow Naomi's deity. (1:15)
34. Showed sorrow. (1:9)

Answer key on page 85

23

ESTHER

Quick Answers

The words you need to solve this puzzle are highlighted in bold below.

WHO

Who Wrote It?

It is not clear who wrote this book. Some say it was **Ezra**, while others suggest **Mordecai**. And still others say it was scribes of the synagogue. Because the book has so many details about Persian life, some believe that the writer used official state documents as a source.

Who's in It?

King Xerxes, Queen **Vashti**, Esther and her Uncle Mordecai, Haman

WHAT

The amazing story in the book of Esther was set in motion when the king's wife, Vashti, refused to parade her beauty in front of her drunken husband and "the people and nobles" (1:11). An irate King Xerxes **disowned** Vashti and sought another queen. His search for a new queen led him to Esther, a Jewish orphan girl, and she became the new queen. Later, the king's right-hand man **Haman** tricked Xerxes into proclaiming an **edict** condemning all Jews to death. It was only when Esther bravely entered the king's presence and asked him to reverse his decree that the Jewish people were **saved** from annihilation.

WHEN

The story of Esther takes place between the years of 464 BC and 435 BC.

WHERE

This story took place in the capital city of **Susa**, where the King of Persia lived, while some of the Israelites were still exiled in the land. Susa was located in what is present-day **Iran**, near its western border. The Jewish people in this book had chosen not to return to Jerusalem when others went back under the leadership of **Zerubbabel** and Ezra. Some would later return with Nehemiah. Esther herself would have been considered an **exile**, since she was Jewish.

WHY

The book of Esther demonstrates God's commitment to work behind the scenes to **protect** His people and to **preserve** His plan. **Disaster** seems imminent in this book, yet in the end God's purposes and plans move forward. For an exiled Jew such as Esther to become queen of Persia seems outrageous. For her people to be threatened by an incontrovertible law made the annihilation of the Jews seem certain. For the queen to address the king as Esther did without losing her head was not expected. And for the king to find a way to save the Jews when everyone knew the laws of the Medes and Persians couldn't be broken was truly **miraculous**. God's name is not mentioned, but His hand is clearly **evident**.

```
L C R I L X P R E S E R V E V
R B X Y I B K C Y E I M K K J
S N S L G F F T V E H T N V B
Z Q F U G R Z C X H D M A A M
S R H Q O P K I L H Y C R C I
M W N W M Y L D Y L U J I Z R
V X T O O E E E U E W P N K A
H W X J R F V Q Y H R R M D C
Z X F E D U V V Z P H O N E U
E O P B E V I D E N T T P N L
R X C H C T E I G F G E K W O
U E M O A M K J Z N R C V O U
B R T S I D B Q O F N T A S S
B K D S P Q C G Q E F Q F I H
A I E H A L A R Z E A P D D B
B V P T S W V L U E L M N S
E O A S G M I Z D P S Q L O X
L Q S S T H Z D N A M A H L E
N Z A T U V A S H T I I M T B
Q Y C J R S D E Y C A D F D I
```

Answer key on page 85

27

Top 10 Key Facts about the Book of Esther

The words you need to solve this puzzle are highlighted in bold below.

1. The incidents described in the book of Esther fit in the chronology of the book of **Ezra**, between chapters six and seven. The events take place about thirty years before the events of Nehemiah begin. Both the book of Esther and the first chapter of Nehemiah take place in **Babylon** (then controlled by **Persia**).
2. A major Jewish special day was created to commemorate the events of Esther's day—especially her **courage** in saving the Jewish nation from being killed off. The day, which is celebrated in Jewish homes in mid-March, is called the Feast of **Purim**.
3. You could call Esther by the name **Myrtle**, which is the meaning of her Hebrew name.
4. Or you could call her **Star**, for that is the meaning of her Persian name: Esther.
5. Esther was of the tribe of **Benjamin**.
6. Before Esther went before King **Xerxes** when he was looking for a replacement for his banished queen, she underwent a year-long beauty **makeover**.
7. After Esther became **queen**, she reigned for thirteen years.
8. The **name of God** is not mentioned in the book of Esther. Also, Esther is not quoted anywhere in the New Testament.
9. The entire plan of God for the **salvation** of sinners depended on Esther's **rescue** of her people. If the king had carried through on his determination to **exterminate** the Jews, the line leading to Jesus would have been permanently broken.
10. Two books of the Bible are named after **women**: Ruth and Esther.

```
E T A N I M R E T X E U M D T
S J Q B U Y F V A R E S C U E
V E G W C C Z U Q M H T S N C
U F X B A Y K N W M Z R E H N
M B I R O Y H J E P T W H A C
N O U B E S N U N O V W O Y J
O R B X P X D O W F F I X N A
I M X J X E G L L H G U E I K
T G D Q R P E I M Y N B C M R
A T O P U R I M Q E B G I A E
V D G K R A I L E W Z A Y J V
L N F R Q I H U W E Q R B N O
A G O X D S Q E Z K P U A E E
S O E L T R Y M K F Y T T B K
G N M Y J E E G A R U O C H A
G C A R C P N S N O C V E S M
S D N A S T A R D E A P O Z Z
Y B X J U A Y A X Q M G B G D
H W Y S S U L U F Q A O L R C
U C N R H S C D S I B X W A M
```

Esther

Queen Vashti Deposed

1 This is what happened during the time of Xerxes, the Xerxes who ruled over 127 provinces stretching from India to Cush: ²At that time King Xerxes reigned from his royal throne in the citadel of Susa, ³and in the third year of his reign he gave a banquet for all his nobles and officials. The military leaders of Persia and Media, the princes, and the nobles of the provinces were present.

⁴For a full 180 days he displayed the vast wealth of his kingdom and the splendor and glory of his majesty. ⁵When these days were over, the king gave a banquet, lasting seven days, in the enclosed garden of the king's palace, for all the people from the least to the greatest who were in the citadel of Susa. ⁶The garden had hangings of white and blue linen, fastened with cords of white linen and purple material to silver rings on marble pillars. There were couches of gold and silver on a mosaic pavement of porphyry, marble, mother-of-pearl and other costly stones. ⁷Wine was served in goblets of gold, each one different from the other, and the royal wine was abundant, in keeping with the king's liberality. ⁸By the king's command each guest was allowed to drink with no restrictions, for the king instructed all the wine stewards to serve each man what he wished.

⁹Queen Vashti also gave a banquet for the women in the royal palace of King Xerxes.

¹⁰On the seventh day, when King Xerxes was in high spirits from wine, he commanded the seven eunuchs who served him — Mehuman, Biztha, Harbona, Bigtha, Abagtha, Zethar and Karkas — ¹¹to bring before him Queen Vashti, wearing her royal crown, in order to display her beauty to the people and nobles, for she was lovely to look at. ¹²But when the attendants delivered the king's command, Queen Vashti refused to come. Then the king became furious and burned with anger.

¹³Since it was customary for the king to consult experts in matters of law and justice, he spoke with the wise men who understood the times ¹⁴and were closest to the king — Karshena, Shethar, Admatha, Tarshish, Meres, Marsena and Memukan, the seven nobles of Persia and Media who had special access to the king and were highest in the kingdom.

Persian banquets were famously extravagant, sometimes lasting for months.

```
B A N Q U E T P G E A J H E N E E M S
N N Q Z F B B R H U S D X P A S H S E
E D D V N U Q O Z R N L X C I C T P X
V I U E R T R V Z S H K J W R Q L O R
E J T F R C L I W C H J D O A Z A B E
S V O Z S D P N O G Z Z W H D C E E X
L X U R G A D C D U S N U Z Q I W U B
D W D G O B L E T S S C E S Q T L A F
Y Y F Z L M W S T X I Y K E Y A Y U Q
B F V X D E S U F E R H L N E D R A G
O J O E X P E R T S Z P C S K E G L L
P N V O C K M X G J R C P N A L E Y I
Y R A T I L I M T U O V I V A S H T I
I E T Z Y N S A P S I R Y A R Y S T E
K R Y E C O V K N L D O M L C M E L N
```

1. The story of Esther takes place during the time of _ _ _ _ _ _. (1:1)
2. The king ruled over 127 _ _ _ _ _ _ _ _ _ _ stretching from India to Cush. (1:1)
3. His royal throne was in the _ _ _ _ _ _ _ _ of Susa. (1:2)
4. The king gave a _ _ _ _ _ _ _ _ _ for all his nobles and officials. (1:3)
5. The _ _ _ _ _ _ _ _ _ leaders of Persia and Media were present. (1:3)
6. For 180 days he displayed the vast _ _ _ _ _ _ _ of his kingdom. (1:4)
7. After this time, the king gave a banquet lasting _ _ _ _ _ _ days. (1:5)
8. The banquet was held in the enclosed _ _ _ _ _ _ _ of the king's palace. (1:5)
9. The hangings were fastened with cords of white linen and _ _ _ _ _ _ _ material. (1:6)

10. The couches were of _ _ _ _ _ and silver on a mosaic pavement. (1:6)
11. The _ _ _ _ _ _ _ _ were made of gold, each one different from the other. (1:7)
12. The king commanded that each guest was allowed to _ _ _ _ _ _ with no restrictions. (1:8)
13. Queen _ _ _ _ _ _ _ _ also gave a banquet for the women. (1:9)
14. King Xerxes commanded that Queen Vashti be brought wearing her royal _ _ _ _ _ _. (1:11)
15. Queen Vashti _ _ _ _ _ _ _ _ _ to come before the king. (1:12)
16. The king became _ _ _ _ _ _ _ _ _ and burned with anger. (1:12)
17. It was customary for the king to consult _ _ _ _ _ _ _ _ in matters of law and justice. (1:13)
18. He spoke with the _ _ _ _ men who understood the times. (1:13)

Answer key on page 85

¹⁵"According to law, what must be done to Queen Vashti?" he asked. "She has not obeyed the command of King Xerxes that the eunuchs have taken to her."

¹⁶Then Memukan replied in the presence of the king and the nobles, "Queen Vashti has done wrong, not only against the king but also against all the nobles and the peoples of all the provinces of King Xerxes. ¹⁷For the queen's conduct will become known to all the women, and so they will despise their husbands and say, 'King Xerxes commanded Queen Vashti to be brought before him, but she would not come.' ¹⁸This very day the Persian and Median women of the nobility who have heard about the queen's conduct will respond to all the king's nobles in the same way. There will be no end of disrespect and discord.

¹⁹"Therefore, if it pleases the king, let him issue a royal decree and let it be written in the laws of Persia and Media, which cannot be repealed, that Vashti is never again to enter the presence of King Xerxes. Also let the king give her royal position to someone else who is better than she. ²⁰Then when the king's edict is proclaimed throughout all his vast realm, all the women will respect their husbands, from the least to the greatest."

²¹The king and his nobles were pleased with this advice, so the king did as Memukan proposed. ²²He sent dispatches to all parts of the kingdom, to each province in its own script and to each people in their own language, proclaiming that every man should be ruler over his own household, using his native tongue.

Esther Made Queen

2 Later when King Xerxes' fury had subsided, he remembered Vashti and what she had done and what he had decreed about her. ²Then the king's personal attendants proposed, "Let a search be made for beautiful young virgins for the king. ³Let the king appoint commissioners in every province of his realm to bring all these beautiful young women into the harem at the citadel of Susa. Let them be placed under the care of Hegai, the king's eunuch, who is in charge of the women; and let beauty treatments be given to them. ⁴Then let the young woman who pleases the king be queen instead of Vashti." This advice appealed to the king, and he followed it.

⁵Now there was in the citadel of Susa a Jew of the tribe of Benjamin, named Mordecai son of Jair, the son of Shimei, the son of Kish, ⁶who had been carried into exile from Jerusalem by Nebuchadnezzar king of Babylon, among those taken captive with Jehoiachin king of Judah. ⁷Mordecai had a cousin named Hadassah, whom he had brought up because she had neither father nor mother. This young woman, who was also known as Esther, had a lovely figure and was beautiful. Mordecai had taken her as his own daughter when her father and mother died.

"Hadassah" means "myrtle" in Hebrew, while "Esther" means "star" in Persian.

```
G N Z K N A Q G B E A U T I F U L N J
Y Y I U V S M S N Q E Y U B M V K X P
N P F O H S D O C O F B Z S C M O L E
N I M A J N E B R M R O D D E X I L E
Q B S Y T Z D D B D Y W R J N A P A V
O N Z O Z V B D T R E A T M E N T S K
V O X Y P N P I W J H C D E Y E B O J
R B N O R A B S D B A P A K E D I C T
E I X O P M C P L M S F C I Z G R N D
H L C R R Q U A Y R S E J N Z Y E E U
T I M E R A H T G G A B K I Q E C Y D
S T C L V F J C O N D U C T U R X X Z
E Y M U U Y O H X E A F B Q E Y Z J E
D I S R E S P E C T H K I E N O R V R
M J Y N P R E S E N C E K M O N O I J
```

1. Queen Vashti had not _ _ _ _ _ _ _ _ the command of King Xerxes. (1:15)
2. Memukan said Vashti had done _ _ _ _ _ _ against the king and the nobles. (1:16)
3. He feared the queen's _ _ _ _ _ _ _ _ _ would be known to all women. (1:17)
4. The women of the _ _ _ _ _ _ _ _ _ _ would respond to the king's nobles in the same way. (1:18)
5. He says there would be no end of _ _ _ _ _ _ _ _ _ _ _ and discord. (1:18)
6. They advised the king to issue a _ _ _ _ _ _ _. (1:19)
7. Vashti may never again enter the _ _ _ _ _ _ _ _ _ of Xerxes. (1:19)
8. The king's _ _ _ _ _ _ was to be proclaimed throughout his realm. (1:20)
9. The king sent _ _ _ _ _ _ _ _ _ _ _ to all parts of the kingdom. (1:22)
10. The king declared that every man was to be _ _ _ _ _ _ over his own household. (1:22)
11. Later, when the king's _ _ _ _ _ had subsided, he remembered Vashti. (2:1)
12. _ _ _ _ _ _ _ _ _ _ young women would be brought for the king. (2:3)
13. They would be placed in the _ _ _ _ _ _ at the citadel of Susa. (2:3)
14. They would receive beauty _ _ _ _ _ _ _ _ _ _. (2:3)
15. The young woman who pleased the king would become _ _ _ _ _ _. (2:4)
16. There was in Susa a Jew of the tribe of _ _ _ _ _ _ _ _ _. (2:5)
17. His name was _ _ _ _ _ _ _ _ _, son of Jair. (2:5)
18. Mordecai's family had been carried into _ _ _ _ _ from Jerusalem. (2:6)
19. Mordecai's cousin was named _ _ _ _ _ _ _ _ _. (2:7)
20. She was also called _ _ _ _ _ _. (2:7)

Answer key on page 86

⁸When the king's order and edict had been proclaimed, many young women were brought to the citadel of Susa and put under the care of Hegai. Esther also was taken to the king's palace and entrusted to Hegai, who had charge of the harem. ⁹She pleased him and won his favor. Immediately he provided her with her beauty treatments and special food. He assigned to her seven female attendants selected from the king's palace and moved her and her attendants into the best place in the harem.

¹⁰Esther had not revealed her nationality and family background, because Mordecai had forbidden her to do so. ¹¹Every day he walked back and forth near the courtyard of the harem to find out how Esther was and what was happening to her.

¹²Before a young woman's turn came to go in to King Xerxes, she had to complete twelve months of beauty treatments prescribed for the women, six months with oil of myrrh and six with perfumes and cosmetics. ¹³And this is how she would go to the king: Anything she wanted was given her to take with her from the harem to the king's palace. ¹⁴In the evening she would go there and in the morning return to another part of the harem to the care of Shaashgaz, the king's eunuch who was in charge of the concubines. She would not return to the king unless he was pleased with her and summoned her by name.

¹⁵When the turn came for Esther (the young woman Mordecai had adopted, the daughter of his uncle Abihail) to go to the king, she asked for nothing other than what Hegai, the king's eunuch who was in charge of the harem, suggested. And Esther won the favor of everyone who saw her. ¹⁶She was taken to King Xerxes in the royal residence in the tenth month, the month of Tebeth, in the seventh year of his reign.

¹⁷Now the king was attracted to Esther more than to any of the other women, and she won his favor and approval more than any of the other virgins. So he set a royal crown on her head and made her queen instead of Vashti. ¹⁸And the king gave a great banquet, Esther's banquet, for all his nobles and officials. He proclaimed a holiday throughout the provinces and distributed gifts with royal liberality.

Mordecai Uncovers a Conspiracy

¹⁹When the virgins were assembled a second time, Mordecai was sitting at the king's gate. ²⁰But Esther had kept secret her family background and nationality just as Mordecai had told her to do, for she continued to follow Mordecai's instructions as she had done when he was bringing her up.

²¹During the time Mordecai was sitting at the king's gate, Bigthana and Teresh, two of the king's officers who guarded the doorway, became angry and conspired to assassinate King Xerxes. ²²But Mordecai found out about the plot and told Queen Esther, who in turn reported it to the king, giving credit to Mordecai. ²³And when the report was investigated and found to be true, the two officials were impaled on poles. All this was recorded in the book of the annals in the presence of the king.

Esther's beauty treatments were elaborate versions of common Persian cosmetic practices.

```
D N O U M Q C E S I W Y R I B E Y U Z
R V X N E R C M A Z Y P E N F T P Y Z
A T U H W A K Z N T A Q L H U Q M M V
Y E B P L F I Q N Y D Q G A R Q O Z A
T T U A P N G Y A Z I F E U G R E Q Y
R A P R Q S E S L Z L B Z E D B Y P T
U N D S X P E M S S O E H E T T R M I
O I Z M G F B W O Y H B C J V P X E L
C S F A V O R V L W K A R U F U W M A
S S C Z Y U F P D L I B A N Q U E T N
R A E C N E D I S E R J H N E X Z R O
I S Q C R O W N A I L E D E L A P M I
M S Z H R T D Z A W D P D E D U Y Z T
J A O M J J N S D E T C A R T T A E A
E T A G W F X L R C U K W V O U U A N
```

1. The king's _____ and edict were proclaimed. (2:8)
2. Many young ___ were brought to the citadel of Susa. (2:8)
3. Esther was taken to the king's _____. (2:8)
4. Hegai provided her with _____ treatments. (2:9)
5. Esther had not revealed her _____ and family background. (2:10)
6. Mordecai walked back and forth near the _____ of the harem. (2:11)
7. The women received six months of beauty treatments with oil of _____. (2:12)
8. Esther won the _____ of everyone who saw her. (2:15)
9. She was taken to the king's royal _____. (2:16)
10. The king was _____ to Esther more than any of the other women. (2:17)
11. The king placed a royal _____ on Esther's head. (2:17)
12. The king gave a great _____ in Esther's honor. (2:18)
13. He proclaimed a _____ throughout the provinces. (2:18)
14. Mordecai was sitting at the king's _____. (2:21)
15. Mordecai overheard a plot to _____ King Xerxes. (2:21)
16. Queen Esther told the king about the plot, giving credit to _____. (2:22)
17. The officials were _____ on poles. (2:23)
18. The report was recorded in the book of the _____. (2:23)

Haman's Plot to Destroy the Jews

3 After these events, King Xerxes honored Haman son of Hammedatha, the Agagite, elevating him and giving him a seat of honor higher than that of all the other nobles. ²All the royal officials at the king's gate knelt down and paid honor to Haman, for the king had commanded this concerning him. But Mordecai would not kneel down or pay him honor.

³Then the royal officials at the king's gate asked Mordecai, "Why do you disobey the king's command?" ⁴Day after day they spoke to him but he refused to comply. Therefore they told Haman about it to see whether Mordecai's behavior would be tolerated, for he had told them he was a Jew.

⁵When Haman saw that Mordecai would not kneel down or pay him honor, he was enraged. ⁶Yet having learned who Mordecai's people were, he scorned the idea of killing only Mordecai. Instead Haman looked for a way to destroy all Mordecai's people, the Jews, throughout the whole kingdom of Xerxes.

⁷In the twelfth year of King Xerxes, in the first month, the month of Nisan, the *pur* (that is, the lot) was cast in the presence of Haman to select a day and month. And the lot fell on the twelfth month, the month of Adar.

⁸Then Haman said to King Xerxes, "There is a certain people dispersed among the peoples in all the provinces of your kingdom who keep themselves separate. Their customs are different from those of all other people, and they do not obey the king's laws; it is not in the king's best interest to tolerate them. ⁹If it pleases the king, let a decree be issued to destroy them, and I will give ten thousand talents of silver to the king's administrators for the royal treasury."

¹⁰So the king took his signet ring from his finger and gave it to Haman son of Hammedatha, the Agagite, the enemy of the Jews. ¹¹"Keep the money," the king said to Haman, "and do with the people as you please."

¹²Then on the thirteenth day of the first month the royal secretaries were summoned. They wrote out in the script of each province and in the language of each people all Haman's orders to the king's satraps, the governors of the various provinces and the nobles of the various peoples. These were written in the name of King Xerxes himself and sealed with his own ring. ¹³Dispatches were sent by couriers to all the king's provinces with the order to destroy, kill and annihilate all the Jews — young and old, women and children — on a single day, the thirteenth day of the twelfth month, the month of Adar, and to plunder their goods. ¹⁴A copy of the text of the edict was to be issued as law in every province and made known to the people of every nationality so they would be ready for that day.

¹⁵The couriers went out, spurred on by the king's command, and the edict was issued in the citadel of Susa. The king and Haman sat down to drink, but the city of Susa was bewildered.

Esther hid her nationality because Jews were often treated badly in Persia.

```
D S A N A F P E H R S X S T E N G I S
M X C O C U T W A P E B V W W Q N L C
B B A S C O R N E D J D K C Z J E T S
O N D B D V F K D C F W N V R E Z D R
E S A Q Q Y U I I G G T N U N R O L E
T L S M Q S Z H C U Y N U K L X D C I
A O X E A K I C T P T S I T K P E N R
L F R T J H S E I R A T E R C E S O U
I F T A G G O N U U L I D S Y Y T S O
H I J R L K N I R D E S D Z E Z R F C
I C T E W A C R Z J N E B I B Q O D Z
N I O L X L T H F A T Z S G O W Y R H
N A Z O X U O F S W S W Y W S G N E E
A L L T U H D U J I V X D C I P U R S
E S W Y R T S P E N R A G E D K J L J
```

1. King Xerxes honored _ _ _ _ _, son of Hammedatha. (3:1)
2. The royal _ _ _ _ _ _ _ _ _ _ knelt down and paid honor to Haman. (3:2)
3. Mordecai would not _ _ _ _ _ down or pay Haman honor. (3:2)
4. Some asked him, "Why do you _ _ _ _ _ _ _ _ the king's command?" (3:3)
5. Haman was _ _ _ _ _ _ _ _ when Mordecai would not pay him honor (3:5)
6. Haman _ _ _ _ _ _ _ _ the idea of killing only Mordecai. (3:6)
7. He wanted to _ _ _ _ _ _ _ _ all of Mordecai's people, the Jews. (3:6)
8. The _ _ _ (that is, the lot) was cast in Haman's presence to select a date. (3:7)
9. Haman said it was not in the king's best interest to _ _ _ _ _ _ _ _ _ the Jews. (3:8)
10. Haman offered ten thousand _ _ _ _ _ _ _ _ of silver to the royal treasury. (3:9)

11. The king took off his _ _ _ _ _ _ _ ring and gave it to Haman. (3:10)
12. The royal _ _ _ _ _ _ _ _ _ _ _ were summoned to write the decree. (3:12)
13. The orders were sealed with the king's own _ _ _ _ _. (3:12)
14. Dispatches were sent by _ _ _ _ _ _ _ _ to all the king's provinces. (3:13)
15. The order was given to destroy, kill, and _ _ _ _ _ _ _ _ _ _ the Jews. (3:13)
16. The order allowed people to _ _ _ _ _ _ _ _ the goods of the Jews. (3:13)
17. The _ _ _ _ _ _ was issued as law in every province. (3:14)
18. The king and Haman sat down to _ _ _ _ _ after the decree was issued. (3:15)
19. The city of _ _ _ _ was bewildered by the king's command. (3:15)

Answer key on page 86

Mordecai Persuades Esther to Help

4 When Mordecai learned of all that had been done, he tore his clothes, put on sackcloth and ashes, and went out into the city, wailing loudly and bitterly. ²But he went only as far as the king's gate, because no one clothed in sackcloth was allowed to enter it. ³In every province to which the edict and order of the king came, there was great mourning among the Jews, with fasting, weeping and wailing. Many lay in sackcloth and ashes.

⁴When Esther's eunuchs and female attendants came and told her about Mordecai, she was in great distress. She sent clothes for him to put on instead of his sackcloth, but he would not accept them. ⁵Then Esther summoned Hathak, one of the king's eunuchs assigned to attend her, and ordered him to find out what was troubling Mordecai and why.

⁶So Hathak went out to Mordecai in the open square of the city in front of the king's gate. ⁷Mordecai told him everything that had happened to him, including the exact amount of money Haman had promised to pay into the royal treasury for the destruction of the Jews. ⁸He also gave him a copy of the text of the edict for their annihilation, which had been published in Susa, to show to Esther and explain it to her, and he told him to instruct her to go into the king's presence to beg for mercy and plead with him for her people.

⁹Hathak went back and reported to Esther what Mordecai had said. ¹⁰Then she instructed him to say to Mordecai, ¹¹"All the king's officials and the people of the royal provinces know that for any man or woman who approaches the king in the inner court without being summoned the king has but one law: that they be put to death unless the king extends the gold scepter to them and spares their lives. But thirty days have passed since I was called to go to the king."

¹²When Esther's words were reported to Mordecai, ¹³he sent back this answer: "Do not think that because you are in the king's house you alone of all the Jews will escape. ¹⁴For if you remain silent at this time, relief and deliverance for the Jews will arise from another place, but you and your father's family will perish. And who knows but that you have come to your royal position for such a time as this?"

¹⁵Then Esther sent this reply to Mordecai: ¹⁶"Go, gather together all the Jews who are in Susa, and fast for me. Do not eat or drink for three days, night or day. I and my attendants will fast as you do. When this is done, I will go to the king, even though it is against the law. And if I perish, I perish."

¹⁷So Mordecai went away and carried out all of Esther's instructions.

Since Haman selected the date for the Jews' destruction by casting the pur (a Persian practice of casting lots), the day of their deliverance is called "Purim."

```
A M T B V Y Y S O A W E V L Z E F D Z
S N X K B Z E G S A C K C L O T H W H
U O E Y U H N U B E B G E D E T P S Q
M I F Q L S O C I W R D S E M E M V E
M T O T E A M W S U X T N V F R O R Q
O I A U P E R I S H U G S U M D Y P G
N S J B Z C N U P U S G E I M X L L N
E O A N N I H I L A T I O N D D R D I
D P R E S E N C E N Q V S F D V E C N
Z F V S F R C G E J C P X K R T S R
B D T A A Y L L Z Y E S C A P E T S U
A G S T G H I W C P K J K D E U I L O
W T H X H S X R T Q E N T E R K B P M
V R E H T A G E V W S F I C Y H N C G
M C I N S T R U C T I O N S T O Y N O
```

1. Mordecai tore his clothes and put on _____ and ashes. (4:1)
2. He went out into the city, wailing loudly and _____. (4:1)
3. No one clothed in sackcloth was allowed to _____ the king's gate. (4:2)
4. There was great _____ among the Jews. (4:3)
5. Esther was in great _____ when she heard about Mordecai. (4:4)
6. Mordecai told Hathak about the exact amount of _____ Haman had promised. (4:7)
7. Mordecai sent Esther a copy of the edict for the _____ of the Jews. (4:8)
8. Mordecai instructed Esther to go into the king's _____. (4:8)
9. Esther said that anyone who approached the king without being _____ would be put to death. (4:11)
10. The king had to extend the gold _____ to spare their life. (4:11)
11. Mordecai warned that Esther would not _____ the destruction of the Jews. (4:13)
12. If she remained _____, relief and deliverance would arise from another place. (4:14)
13. Esther may have come to her royal _____ for such a time as this. (4:14)
14. Esther told Mordecai to _____ together all the Jews in Susa. (4:16)
15. She asked them to _____ for her, not eating or drinking for three days. (4:16)
16. Esther said, "If I _____, I perish." (4:16)
17. Mordecai carried out all of Esther's _____. (4:17)

Answer key on page 86

Esther's Request to the King

5 On the third day Esther put on her royal robes and stood in the inner court of the palace, in front of the king's hall. The king was sitting on his royal throne in the hall, facing the entrance. ²When he saw Queen Esther standing in the court, he was pleased with her and held out to her the gold scepter that was in his hand. So Esther approached and touched the tip of the scepter.

³Then the king asked, "What is it, Queen Esther? What is your request? Even up to half the kingdom, it will be given you."

⁴"If it pleases the king," replied Esther, "let the king, together with Haman, come today to a banquet I have prepared for him."

⁵"Bring Haman at once," the king said, "so that we may do what Esther asks."

So the king and Haman went to the banquet Esther had prepared. ⁶As they were drinking wine, the king again asked Esther, "Now what is your petition? It will be given you. And what is your request? Even up to half the kingdom, it will be granted."

⁷Esther replied, "My petition and my request is this: ⁸If the king regards me with favor and if it pleases the king to grant my petition and fulfill my request, let the king and Haman come tomorrow to the banquet I will prepare for them. Then I will answer the king's question."

Haman's Rage Against Mordecai

⁹Haman went out that day happy and in high spirits. But when he saw Mordecai at the king's gate and observed that he neither rose nor showed fear in his presence, he was filled with rage against Mordecai. ¹⁰Nevertheless, Haman restrained himself and went home.

Calling together his friends and Zeresh, his wife, ¹¹Haman boasted to them about his vast wealth, his many sons, and all the ways the king had honored him and how he had elevated him above the other nobles and officials. ¹²"And that's not all," Haman added. "I'm the only person Queen Esther invited to accompany the king to the banquet she gave. And she has invited me along with the king tomorrow. ¹³But all this gives me no satisfaction as long as I see that Jew Mordecai sitting at the king's gate."

¹⁴His wife Zeresh and all his friends said to him, "Have a pole set up, reaching to a height of fifty cubits, and ask the king in the morning to have Mordecai impaled on it. Then go with the king to the banquet and enjoy yourself." This suggestion delighted Haman, and he had the pole set up.

Haman is called an Agagite, meaning he may have been descended from King Agag, an early enemy of the kingdom of Israel.

```
P D H I W V X O T E N N L C U S C A O
U E P O L E E Q T N E E I K H P X V D
T N V E E M Q G E L E V A T E D J H S
D I W L G W E L U C T M O D G N I K C
F A G F A E F V Q Q D P E G K S Y H E
R R G R R A U T N Q W T G T C J H V P
I T T N S L X X A H H I A G O B X P T
E S U J Q T X K B G D W W R O B E S E
N E M B G H Z M I E E I T H R O N E R
D R M O B Y Q L P B L F T O Y K Y I O
S W Q B S S E Q P V A P T X R L T Y H
T H K G C D R U M M P H B Q W R F Z X
S P I R I T S V A J M O H A U O I H Z
O U A A D T D Z O D I F M O V M F U O
N O I T C A F S I T A S C L Z A Q F T
```

1. On the third day, Esther put on her royal _ _ _ _ _. (5:1)
2. She stood in the inner _ _ _ _ _ _ of the palace. (5:1)
3. The king was sitting on his royal _ _ _ _ _ _ _. (5:1)
4. The king was pleased and held out the gold _ _ _ _ _ _ _ _ to Esther. (5:2)
5. The king offered Esther up to half the _ _ _ _ _ _ _ _. (5:3)
6. Esther invited the king and Haman to a _ _ _ _ _ _ _ _ she had prepared for them. (5:4)
7. Haman went out that day happy and in high _ _ _ _ _ _ _ _ _. (5:9)
8. When he saw Mordecai, he was filled with _ _ _ _ _. (5:9)
9. Haman _ _ _ _ _ _ _ _ _ _ _ himself and went home. (5:10)
10. Haman gathered his _ _ _ _ _ _ _ _ and Zeresh, his wife. (5:10)
11. Haman boasted about his vast _ _ _ _ _ _ _. (5:11)
12. He boasted that he had been _ _ _ _ _ _ _ _ _ by the king above the nobles. (5:11)
13. But he had no _ _ _ _ _ _ _ _ _ _ _ _ _ as long as he saw Mordecai at the gate. (5:13)
14. His wife and friends told Haman to have a _ _ _ _ _ set up for Mordecai. (5:14)
15. The pole was to be _ _ _ _ _ _ cubits high. (5:14)
16. Haman would ask to have Mordecai _ _ _ _ _ _ _ _ on the pole. (5:14)
17. This suggestion _ _ _ _ _ _ _ _ _ _ Haman. (5:14)

Answer key on page 86

Mordecai Honored

6 That night the king could not sleep; so he ordered the book of the chronicles, the record of his reign, to be brought in and read to him. ²It was found recorded there that Mordecai had exposed Bigthana and Teresh, two of the king's officers who guarded the doorway, who had conspired to assassinate King Xerxes.

³"What honor and recognition has Mordecai received for this?" the king asked.

"Nothing has been done for him," his attendants answered.

⁴The king said, "Who is in the court?" Now Haman had just entered the outer court of the palace to speak to the king about impaling Mordecai on the pole he had set up for him.

⁵His attendants answered, "Haman is standing in the court."

"Bring him in," the king ordered.

⁶When Haman entered, the king asked him, "What should be done for the man the king delights to honor?"

Now Haman thought to himself, "Who is there that the king would rather honor than me?" ⁷So he answered the king, "For the man the king delights to honor, ⁸have them bring a royal robe the king has worn and a horse the king has ridden, one with a royal crest placed on its head. ⁹Then let the robe and horse be entrusted to one of the king's most noble princes. Let them robe the man the king delights to honor, and lead him on the horse through the city streets, proclaiming before him, 'This is what is done for the man the king delights to honor!'"

¹⁰"Go at once," the king commanded Haman. "Get the robe and the horse and do just as you have suggested for Mordecai the Jew, who sits at the king's gate. Do not neglect anything you have recommended."

¹¹So Haman got the robe and the horse. He robed Mordecai, and led him on horseback through the city streets, proclaiming before him, "This is what is done for the man the king delights to honor!"

¹²Afterward Mordecai returned to the king's gate. But Haman rushed home, with his head covered in grief, ¹³and told Zeresh his wife and all his friends everything that had happened to him.

His advisers and his wife Zeresh said to him, "Since Mordecai, before whom your downfall has started, is of Jewish origin, you cannot stand against him — you will surely come to ruin!" ¹⁴While they were still talking with him, the king's eunuchs arrived and hurried Haman away to the banquet Esther had prepared.

Mordecai's reward marks the beginning of his rise to power, eventually overtaking Haman as the king's second-in-command.

```
O S C O I Z X G H V R S M R B E L W Y
O U E O P J P Z T H O H O L O O V W E
Z D T M U L O F G T Y O W C T N Q S C
H S A S Y R X V J C A N O E E B O C D
R T G O M E T Q S F L N X J U L Y H J
W E S P O N W T U S S T L N Q C B R B
M E A G R U L G E P B M Z X N I G O T
S R P E D X X Y I G R I E F A E V N Z
D T V D E J K R Y E M J G Z B R X I C
B S H C C R E C O G N I T I O N R C L
B Z L G A D P X X Z G Q E O C N F L R
X W D I I Z E T P X K G M A X E F E O
A B U V S L D Q V V D D R U I N V S B
N R H S I W E J P A N N B C B J Y X E
C F J N E H E D B D H G N N N O G F E
```

1. When the king could not sleep, he had the book of the _ _ _ _ _ _ _ _ _ _ read to him. (6:1)

2. Mordecai had exposed the king's officers who had _ _ _ _ _ _ _ _ _ _ to assassinate the king. (6:2)

3. The king asked if Mordecai had received honor and _ _ _ _ _ _ _ _ _ _ _ _ for his deeds. (6:3)

4. Haman had just entered the outer _ _ _ _ _ _ of the palace. (6:4)

5. The king asked Haman, "What should be done for the man the king _ _ _ _ _ _ _ _ to honor?" (6:6)

6. Haman thought, "Who would the king rather _ _ _ _ _ than me?" (6:6)

7. Haman suggested a royal _ _ _ _ _ should be given to the man the king honors. (6:8)

8. A _ _ _ _ _ _ crest would be placed on the honored man's horse. (6:8)

9. The man would be led in honor through the city _ _ _ _ _ _ _ _. (6:9)

10. The king commanded Haman to honor _ _ _ _ _ _ _ _ _ as he had recommended. (6:10)

11. Afterward, Mordecai returned to the king's _ _ _ _ _. (6:12)

12. Haman rushed home, with his head covered in _ _ _ _ _ _. (6:12)

13. His wife and friends told him he would surely come to _ _ _ _ _. (6:13)

14. They said he could not stand against Mordecai because he was of _ _ _ _ _ _ _ origin. (6:13)

15. Haman was hurried to the _ _ _ _ _ _ _ _ Esther had prepared. (6:14)

Answer key on page 86

Haman Impaled

7 So the king and Haman went to Queen Esther's banquet, ²and as they were drinking wine on the second day, the king again asked, "Queen Esther, what is your petition? It will be given you. What is your request? Even up to half the kingdom, it will be granted."

³Then Queen Esther answered, "If I have found favor with you, Your Majesty, and if it pleases you, grant me my life — this is my petition. And spare my people — this is my request. ⁴For I and my people have been sold to be destroyed, killed and annihilated. If we had merely been sold as male and female slaves, I would have kept quiet, because no such distress would justify disturbing the king."

⁵King Xerxes asked Queen Esther, "Who is he? Where is he — the man who has dared to do such a thing?"

⁶Esther said, "An adversary and enemy! This vile Haman!"

Then Haman was terrified before the king and queen. ⁷The king got up in a rage, left his wine and went out into the palace garden. But Haman, realizing that the king had already decided his fate, stayed behind to beg Queen Esther for his life.

⁸Just as the king returned from the palace garden to the banquet hall, Haman was falling on the couch where Esther was reclining.

The king exclaimed, "Will he even molest the queen while she is with me in the house?"

As soon as the word left the king's mouth, they covered Haman's face. ⁹Then Harbona, one of the eunuchs attending the king, said, "A pole reaching to a height of fifty cubits stands by Haman's house. He had it set up for Mordecai, who spoke up to help the king."

The king said, "Impale him on it!" ¹⁰So they impaled Haman on the pole he had set up for Mordecai. Then the king's fury subsided.

The King's Edict in Behalf of the Jews

8 That same day King Xerxes gave Queen Esther the estate of Haman, the enemy of the Jews. And Mordecai came into the presence of the king, for Esther had told how he was related to her. ²The king took off his signet ring, which he had reclaimed from Haman, and presented it to Mordecai. And Esther appointed him over Haman's estate.

³Esther again pleaded with the king, falling at his feet and weeping. She begged him to put an end to the evil plan of Haman the Agagite, which he had devised against the Jews. ⁴Then the king extended the gold scepter to Esther and she arose and stood before him.

The pole Haman set up for killing Mordecai was about 75 feet tall.

```
E N O I T I T E P W Z K E I V F E S N
L S E U C T J J P T H U G N I L L A F
F K I N G D O M T Z C F B L W U C T H
U E V G Q D N I B V M Z A B P M T E H
R L B S N D J U O U X D Q T H X Q U A
Y P G D P E A D V E R S A R Y X S Q D
S O H F Z I T Q N H Q B G R M E Q N X
M E Z P B F D K Y M V D E A E L E A W
Q P B X W I K R K H B X I T E D L B G
Y I R D X R F A C E N C X A A C O D T
C H J G X R O S W I E P Q M V T P S D
B V A F U E X I C A D E Y O R T S E D
O S C E P T E R F L R P C K E W T E E
Z S F K D O M B S F A O W Y G K I L I
W D P J D O N J C H G D E D A E L P V
```

1. The king and Haman went to Queen Esther's _ _ _ _ _ _ _ _. (7:1)
2. The king asked Esther what her _ _ _ _ _ _ _ _ _ was. (7:2)
3. He said he would give her up to half the _ _ _ _ _ _ _. (7:2)
4. Esther pleaded that the king would save her life and spare her _ _ _ _ _ _ _. (7:3)
5. She told him that her people had been sold to be _ _ _ _ _ _ _ _ _ _, killed, and annihilated. (7:4)
6. King Xerxes asked who had _ _ _ _ _ _ to do such a thing. (7:5)
7. Esther called Haman an _ _ _ _ _ _ _ _ _ _ and an enemy. (7:6)
8. Haman was _ _ _ _ _ _ _ _ _ _ _ before the king and queen. (7:6)
9. In a rage, the king went into the palace _ _ _ _ _ _ _. (7:7)

10. When he returned, Haman was _ _ _ _ _ _ _ _ on the couch where Esther was reclining. (7:8)
11. At the king's word, Haman's _ _ _ _ was covered. (7:8)
12. The king learned of the _ _ _ _ Haman had set up for Mordecai. (7:9)
13. After Haman was executed, the king's _ _ _ _ _ subsided. (7:10)
14. King Xerxes gave Haman's _ _ _ _ _ _ _ to Queen Esther. (8:1)
15. The king took off his _ _ _ _ _ _ _ ring and gave it to Mordecai. (8:2)
16. Esther _ _ _ _ _ _ _ _ with the king again, falling at his feet. (8:3)
17. The king extended his gold _ _ _ _ _ _ _ _ to Esther. (8:4)

⁵"If it pleases the king," she said, "and if he regards me with favor and thinks it the right thing to do, and if he is pleased with me, let an order be written overruling the dispatches that Haman son of Hammedatha, the Agagite, devised and wrote to destroy the Jews in all the king's provinces. ⁶For how can I bear to see disaster fall on my people? How can I bear to see the destruction of my family?"

⁷King Xerxes replied to Queen Esther and to Mordecai the Jew, "Because Haman attacked the Jews, I have given his estate to Esther, and they have impaled him on the pole he set up. ⁸Now write another decree in the king's name in behalf of the Jews as seems best to you, and seal it with the king's signet ring—for no document written in the king's name and sealed with his ring can be revoked."

⁹At once the royal secretaries were summoned—on the twenty-third day of the third month, the month of Sivan. They wrote out all Mordecai's orders to the Jews, and to the satraps, governors and nobles of the 127 provinces stretching from India to Cush. These orders were written in the script of each province and the language of each people and also to the Jews in their own script and language. ¹⁰Mordecai wrote in the name of King Xerxes, sealed the dispatches with the king's signet ring, and sent them by mounted couriers, who rode fast horses especially bred for the king.

¹¹The king's edict granted the Jews in every city the right to assemble and protect themselves; to destroy, kill and annihilate the armed men of any nationality or province who might attack them and their women and children, and to plunder the property of their enemies. ¹²The day appointed for the Jews to do this in all the provinces of King Xerxes was the thirteenth day of the twelfth month, the month of Adar. ¹³A copy of the text of the edict was to be issued as law in every province and made known to the people of every nationality so that the Jews would be ready on that day to avenge themselves on their enemies.

¹⁴The couriers, riding the royal horses, went out, spurred on by the king's command, and the edict was issued in the citadel of Susa.

The Triumph of the Jews

¹⁵When Mordecai left the king's presence, he was wearing royal garments of blue and white, a large crown of gold and a purple robe of fine linen. And the city of Susa held a joyous celebration. ¹⁶For the Jews it was a time of happiness and joy, gladness and honor. ¹⁷In every province and in every city to which the edict of the king came, there was joy and gladness among the Jews, with feasting and celebrating. And many people of other nationalities became Jews because fear of the Jews had seized them.

Laws of Media and Persia sealed by the king could not be revoked.

```
J R A S W O N A T I O N A L I T I E S
P S Z T Y P U Y A V F C V K V U X B B
N U L C Y D P D I S P A T C H E S G T
W O D J E O P E T P S N U R X A E I F
O Y G M C V D W D S H S T D I M C G P
R O X G G A R M E N T S O W D T R M H
C J P S O D A M A N H A P P I N E S S
D P E R S V B G E O K U Y O Q F T R H
I P N J O L M M T C C F K E D A A E S
S Q E C E V R N A W L E N E X D R I O
A R M I Q A I T B P L O K R E J I R R
S U I B G U T N S G A O S C W Q E U K
T X E T Y A T X C H V E X E I Y S O Z
E V S N A M N D S E Q D P D B S G C A
R K X S S T S M R K S X D K F V V E Q
```

1. Esther asked the king to overrule the _ _ _ _ _ _ _ _ _ _ _ _ devised by Haman. (8:5)
2. She could not bear to see _ _ _ _ _ _ _ _ fall on her people. (8:6)
3. The king ordered a new _ _ _ _ _ _ _ _ to be written in behalf of the Jews. (8:8)
4. No document written in the king's name and sealed with his ring can be _ _ _ _ _ _ _ _. (8:8)
5. Royal _ _ _ _ _ _ _ _ _ _ _ _ were summoned to write the decree. (8:9)
6. The decree was sent to all 127 _ _ _ _ _ _ _ _ _ _ from India to Cush. (8:9)
7. The king's edict granted Jews the right to _ _ _ _ _ _ _ _ _ and protect themselves. (8:11)
8. The Jews could destroy any armed men who might _ _ _ _ _ _ _ _ them. (8:11)
9. They could plunder the property of their _ _ _ _ _ _ _ _. (8:11)
10. A _ _ _ _ _ of the text of the edict was sent to every province. (8:13)
11. The _ _ _ _ _ _ _ _ _ _ were spurred on by the king's command. (8:14)
12. Mordecai left the king's presence in royal _ _ _ _ _ _ _ _ _. (8:15)
13. He wore a large _ _ _ _ _ _ of gold. (8:15)
14. The city of Susa held a _ _ _ _ _ _ _ celebration. (8:15)
15. The Jews had a time of _ _ _ _ _ _ _ _ _ and joy. (8:16)
16. Many people of other _ _ _ _ _ _ _ _ _ _ _ _ _ _ became Jews. (8:17)

Answer key on page 87

9 On the thirteenth day of the twelfth month, the month of Adar, the edict commanded by the king was to be carried out. On this day the enemies of the Jews had hoped to overpower them, but now the tables were turned and the Jews got the upper hand over those who hated them. ²The Jews assembled in their cities in all the provinces of King Xerxes to attack those determined to destroy them. No one could stand against them, because the people of all the other nationalities were afraid of them. ³And all the nobles of the provinces, the satraps, the governors and the king's administrators helped the Jews, because fear of Mordecai had seized them. ⁴Mordecai was prominent in the palace; his reputation spread throughout the provinces, and he became more and more powerful.

⁵The Jews struck down all their enemies with the sword, killing and destroying them, and they did what they pleased to those who hated them. ⁶In the citadel of Susa, the Jews killed and destroyed five hundred men. ⁷They also killed Parshandatha, Dalphon, Aspatha, ⁸Poratha, Adalia, Aridatha, ⁹Parmashta, Arisai, Aridai and Vaizatha, ¹⁰the ten sons of Haman son of Hammedatha, the enemy of the Jews. But they did not lay their hands on the plunder.

¹¹The number of those killed in the citadel of Susa was reported to the king that same day. ¹²The king said to Queen Esther, "The Jews have killed and destroyed five hundred men and the ten sons of Haman in the citadel of Susa. What have they done in the rest of the king's provinces? Now what is your petition? It will be given you. What is your request? It will also be granted."

¹³"If it pleases the king," Esther answered, "give the Jews in Susa permission to carry out this day's edict tomorrow also, and let Haman's ten sons be impaled on poles."

¹⁴So the king commanded that this be done. An edict was issued in Susa, and they impaled the ten sons of Haman. ¹⁵The Jews in Susa came together on the fourteenth day of the month of Adar, and they put to death in Susa three hundred men, but they did not lay their hands on the plunder.

¹⁶Meanwhile, the remainder of the Jews who were in the king's provinces also assembled to protect themselves and get relief from their enemies. They killed seventy-five thousand of them but did not lay their hands on the plunder. ¹⁷This happened on the thirteenth day of the month of Adar, and on the fourteenth they rested and made it a day of feasting and joy.

¹⁸The Jews in Susa, however, had assembled on the thirteenth and fourteenth, and then on the fifteenth they rested and made it a day of feasting and joy.

¹⁹That is why rural Jews — those living in villages — observe the fourteenth of the month of Adar as a day of joy and feasting, a day for giving presents to each other.

The citadel of Susa was Xerxes' capital in the Persian Empire.

```
B F O G F S C H W S D H N M W B O V U
W C I I X I D H E S M F F H M J E S W
J S I O T N O I T A T U P E R U Q T M
R D O I U V M I U D I Z E W V D M N J
T H E P P E R M I S S I O N R E O E X
C S N V N S P C E M L W W I H A Q S M
O Y E E I A C E D R O M O K I L L E D
M I J O X O B G V S K J T R U A I R F
M E Q W D V G J N O U X C O D E R P E
A A K L E M C I Q Q N S Y W W C A H A
N A B W T A N Z S O S N A M A H A C S
D I H B S C Y W T T H Y I L Y C S L T
E T Y U E E W T A Q I W J I R L D P I
D L D C R E D N U L P O X R G G B Y N
N P Z A O U D T H V P O X T N X J G G
```

1. The _____ of the Jews had hoped to overpower them. (9:1)
2. The Jews assembled in their _____. (9:2)
3. No one could _____ against them. (9:2)
4. The king's nobles and administrators helped the Jews out of fear of _____. (9:3)
5. Mordecai's _____ spread throughout the provinces. (9:4)
6. The Jews struck down their enemies with the _____. (9:5)
7. In the citadel of _____, the Jews killed five hundred men. (9:6)
8. The ten sons of _____ were killed. (9:10)
9. The number of those _____ was reported to the king. (9:11)
10. Esther asked to give the Jews in Susa _____ to carry out the edict the next day also. (9:13)
11. The king _____ that this be done. (9:14)
12. The Jews in Susa did not lay their hands on the _____. (9:15)
13. On the fourteenth day, the Jews _____ and celebrated. (9:17)
14. They made it a day of _____ and joy. (9:17)
15. Rural Jews celebrate the day every year by feasting and giving _____ to each other. (9:19)

Answer key on page 87

Purim Established

²⁰Mordecai recorded these events, and he sent letters to all the Jews throughout the provinces of King Xerxes, near and far, ²¹to have them celebrate annually the fourteenth and fifteenth days of the month of Adar ²²as the time when the Jews got relief from their enemies, and as the month when their sorrow was turned into joy and their mourning into a day of celebration. He wrote them to observe the days as days of feasting and joy and giving presents of food to one another and gifts to the poor.

²³So the Jews agreed to continue the celebration they had begun, doing what Mordecai had written to them. ²⁴For Haman son of Hammedatha, the Agagite, the enemy of all the Jews, had plotted against the Jews to destroy them and had cast the *pur* (that is, the lot) for their ruin and destruction. ²⁵But when the plot came to the king's attention, he issued written orders that the evil scheme Haman had devised against the Jews should come back onto his own head, and that he and his sons should be impaled on poles. ²⁶(Therefore these days were called Purim, from the word *pur*.) Because of everything written in this letter and because of what they had seen and what had happened to them, ²⁷the Jews took it on themselves to establish the custom that they and their descendants and all who join them should without fail observe these two days every year, in the way prescribed and at the time appointed. ²⁸These days should be remembered and observed in every generation by every family, and in every province and in every city. And these days of Purim should never fail to be celebrated by the Jews — nor should the memory of these days die out among their descendants.

²⁹So Queen Esther, daughter of Abihail, along with Mordecai the Jew, wrote with full authority to confirm this second letter concerning Purim. ³⁰And Mordecai sent letters to all the Jews in the 127 provinces of Xerxes' kingdom — words of goodwill and assurance — ³¹to establish these days of Purim at their designated times, as Mordecai the Jew and Queen Esther had decreed for them, and as they had established for themselves and their descendants in regard to their times of fasting and lamentation. ³²Esther's decree confirmed these regulations about Purim, and it was written down in the records.

The Greatness of Mordecai

10 King Xerxes imposed tribute throughout the empire, to its distant shores. ²And all his acts of power and might, together with a full account of the greatness of Mordecai, whom the king had promoted, are they not written in the book of the annals of the kings of Media and Persia? ³Mordecai the Jew was second in rank to King Xerxes, preeminent among the Jews, and held in high esteem by his many fellow Jews, because he worked for the good of his people and spoke up for the welfare of all the Jews.

Jewish communities today still celebrate Purim to commemorate these events.

```
J Q V A C J I P M E R L D M S O Y P O
Z E A N O I T A R B E L E C P T P U Q
N G X A G J V R G P P W S Z I R F R L
S U E W G R R A O J C F A R E G Q I L
Y L L A U N N A Y K H R O E A P K M G
A C B N C P N W F U Q H M S J R Q U Z
N I D N O N R A N K T I T T W O L P T
A D Z A K R D U T U N S H A U V S V E
J T H L K P E R A E N D Q B K I L Q R
F P X S M Y Z C N V D F F L A N U H A
T E T U B I R T O I N S Z I U C K G F
G R C M U F C O N R F Y Z S L E W A L
A A F G U F A B M N D P C H V S Y U E
W C S O R R O W D E I E H V D K W O W
A O S R E D R O R P M I D D A E H D A
```

1. Mordecai _ _ _ _ _ _ _ _ _ these events. (9:20)
2. The Jews were to celebrate _ _ _ _ _ _ _ _ _ the 14th and 15th of the month of Adar. (9:21)
3. They would celebrate because their _ _ _ _ _ _ was turned into joy. (9:22)
4. Their mourning became a day of _ _ _ _ _ _ _ _ _ _ _ _. (9:22)
5. The Jews would give presents to one another and _ _ _ _ _ _ to the poor. (9:22)
6. The king issued written _ _ _ _ _ _ _ against Haman's evil scheme. (9:25)
7. These days of celebration were called _ _ _ _ _ _. (9:26)
8. The Jews decided to _ _ _ _ _ _ _ _ _ _ the custom for future generations. (9:27)
9. The _ _ _ _ _ _ _ of these days should never die out among their descendents. (9:28)
10. Queen Esther and Mordecai wrote with full _ _ _ _ _ _ _ _ _ _. (9:29)
11. Mordecai sent letters to the Jews in all the _ _ _ _ _ _ _ _ _ _. (9:30)
12. King Xerxes imposed _ _ _ _ _ _ _ _ throughout the empire. (10:1)
13. Mordecai's greatness was written in the book of the _ _ _ _ _ _ _. (10:2)
14. Mordecai was second in _ _ _ _ _ to King Xerxes. (10:3)
15. He was _ _ _ _ _ _ _ _ _ _ _ among the Jews. (10:3)
16. He spoke up for the _ _ _ _ _ _ _ _ of all the Jews. (10:3)

Answer key on page 87

Highlights of Esther

The next word search covers the full book of Esther, highlighting some key words and themes from throughout the book.

ANNIHILATE	MORDECAI
BANQUET	NOBLES
BEAUTIFUL	PALACE
CROWN	PETITION
DECREE	PLUNDER
DELIVERANCE	PURIM
DESTRUCTION	QUEEN
ESTHER	RAGE
FAST	SACKCLOTH
FAVOR	SCEPTER
HAMAN	SIGNET RING
HONOR	SUSA
IMPALED	THRONE
JEWS	VASHTI
KINGDOM	XERXES

```
L V K E Q E N H W C M O R D E C A I Q
K P E A R B V G F V R I L N Y H Z U Y
S G S J M E B H C T J E Q O J Q E E Y
B U O L S A C K C L O T H I Q E I E H
S L R R S U C I Y W O K V T N C M R E
R T R R K T R N N I T Z A I S J P C R
Y I A T V I X G G V E H S T N E A E E
C R O W N F G D Q S U G H E F L L D T
R K H L I U N O J I Q O T P A N E J P
L E J E F L I M X N N F I P M I D N E
C Z K A Q V R V A O A X Q G M P G U C
C X T N F Y T L R M B B S E L B O N S
J X L W G W E O A A X P U R I M Y Z N
R M I W M Y N K J J G C K O Y U V U Y
W N F U S P G B H W Z E M V M Q A D D
T H S W A B I G A N N I H I L A T E G
Z R E Z H P S T K A T H R O N E U J H
Q J M N I C R N O P Z P J X F A V O R
D E L I V E R A N C E X L N S Q O S C
P M J B T P T M V J G E K U H G V C X
L W J P S U Q A F T S R X L N J O Q P
J I N O A G A H A K U X C M H D P U A
Y Y O J F V L N U Z M E C I O U E U T
T H V N O I T C U R T S E D E Y P R M
I C O N B U M Y I M L M W U K D K R J
```

Esther

ACROSS

1. Seal that authorized royal decrees. (3:10)
6. The king's eunuch in charge of the harem. (2:8)
7. Royal declaration. (1:19)
10. Activity on a day of celebration. (9:17)
11. Royal position given to Esther. (2:17)
13. Reaction of Jews to second decree. (8:16)
14. Son of Jair. (2:5)
15. Completely destroy. (8:11)
20. The enemy Haman. (7:6)
22. 127 territories in Xerxes' kingdom. (1:1)
25. Property of Haman given to Esther. (8:1)
27. Garment of mourning. (4:1)
28. Royal garment worn as a sign of honor. (6:8)
30. Festival commemorating the Jews' deliverance. (9:26)
31. King who ruled from India to Cush. (1:1)
32. What Esther might do for approaching the king. (4:16)
33. Event prepared by Esther for Xerxes and Haman. (7:1)
34. Young woman made queen to replace Vashti. (2:7)
35. Fate planned for the Jews. (4:7)

DOWN

2. Emotion filling Haman at Mordecai's disregard. (5:9)
3. Book recording Mordecai's good deed. (6:1)
4. Future generations who will observe Purim. (9:28)
5. Esther's request to the King. (5:6)
6. Respect Mordecai would not pay to Haman. (3:2)
8. Haman's role to the Jews. (7:6)
9. Esther's Hebrew name. (2:7)
10. Approval won from everyone who saw Esther. (2:15)
12. Agagite elevated above other nobles. (3:1)
14. What should never die out among the Jews. (9:28)
16. Executed on a pole. (7:10)
17. Lot cast to select day of destruction. (3:7)
18. Golden object extended to spare Queen Esther. (5:2)
19. Spoil untouched by the Jews. (9:10)
21. Three-day preparation of Esther and the Jews. (4:16)
23. Queen who refused the king's command. (1:12)
24. Festive response to Jews' deliverance. (8:15)
26. Haman's ethnic identity. (3:1)
29. Mordecai's people. (3:6)
30. Fifty-cubit structure built for Mordecai's execution. (5:14)
32. Assassination conspiracy discovered by Mordecai. (2:22)

Answer key on page 88

55

SONG OF SONGS

Quick Answers

The words you need to solve this puzzle are highlighted in bold below.

WHO

Who Wrote It?

The first verse of this book starts: "Solomon's Song of Songs." That is a good indication that the **wise man** himself penned this book.

Who's in It?

The Shulammite woman, a **chorus**, Solomon

WHAT

Is this book simply about the **romantic** relationship between a man and a woman, or is it an **allegory** for our relationship with God? Some have suggested that it is the actual love story between Solomon and a woman. Others see it as an allegory for the **union** between **Christ** and the **church**—or between Christ and an individual He is working to win to **faith**.

WHEN

Solomon lived in the 900s BC, which puts Song of Solomon's completion date during the same time period the first **temple** was constructed.

WHERE

The book has plenty of geographic references, which could apply if it is an actual **depiction** of a love story. In other words, some see the Song of Songs as an allegory and that the characters are **representatives** of something else—for instance, the **bridegroom** is Christ and the bride is the church. Or it could be seen as a true **love story** between two real people. If that is the case, the geographic references are places related to those real people.

WHY

This is one of the key questions relating to this book and its **unique** subject matter in the canon of Scripture. Some say it is **wisdom** literature that gives the reader information about how a man and woman are to properly live and love in a spousal relationship. It has been suggested that the book was intended for use in **wedding** ceremonies. As mentioned, some also believe it is an allegory for the love relationship between God and His people.

H	C	R	U	H	C	C	K	S	G	S	T	K	K	S
I	G	T	N	S	T	E	Y	U	Y	F	E	I	Z	E
Q	M	K	I	Q	I	M	R	R	B	N	M	X	Z	V
T	Y	L	O	V	E	S	T	O	R	Y	P	T	P	I
V	Y	F	N	L	H	E	M	H	I	X	L	N	N	T
Z	F	B	N	D	W	U	P	C	R	C	E	A	E	A
U	A	Z	K	X	E	Q	I	K	O	A	J	J	Z	T
X	I	R	X	P	D	I	N	A	M	E	S	I	W	N
U	T	R	S	X	D	N	X	X	A	P	U	Q	V	E
M	H	E	U	I	I	U	T	K	N	N	N	Z	X	S
W	O	J	O	T	N	D	P	J	T	O	H	Z	S	E
U	Y	O	A	F	G	K	K	Z	I	I	U	A	J	R
H	L	R	R	T	S	I	R	H	C	T	X	H	Z	P
Z	M	P	O	G	B	C	B	K	R	C	T	V	D	E
S	O	F	H	G	E	I	P	G	L	I	I	A	R	R
D	D	Q	W	F	E	D	G	U	A	P	A	K	Y	N
R	S	W	Z	C	A	L	I	K	M	E	D	Q	G	C
G	I	G	W	T	V	D	L	R	P	D	E	F	Y	Q
D	W	R	A	E	L	S	K	A	B	V	K	Z	X	W
P	S	G	I	V	E	O	U	T	A	G	H	O	R	Q

Answer key on page 88

Top 10 Key Facts about Song of Songs

The words you need to solve this puzzle are highlighted in bold below.

1. Song of Songs is one of the two Bible books that don't mention the name of God.
2. This is unlike any other book of the Bible in its straightforward portrayal of the love **relationship** between a man and a woman.
3. Song of Songs is the only book in the Bible that consists of a single **poem**.
4. The book contains a number of interesting figures of speech to describe the love relationship between a man and a woman. For example: "Your **love** is more delightful than **wine**" (1:2), "your eyes are **doves**" (1:15), "my beloved is like a **gazelle**" (2:9), and, surprisingly, "your hair is like a flock of **goats**" (4:1).
5. Song of Songs mentions more than twenty **plant** species and more than a dozen **animals**.
6. There is some **geography** in this book as well: Chapter 1: Jerusalem, Kedar, En Gedi. Chapter 2: Sharon, Jerusalem. Chapter 3: Jerusalem (Zion), Lebanon. Chapter 4: **Gilead**, Lebanon, Amana, Hermon. Chapter 5: Jerusalem, Lebanon. Chapter 6: Tirzah, Gilead, Shulem. Chapter 7: Heshbon, Bath Rabbim, Damascus, **Mount Carmel**. Chapter 8: Jerusalem, Baal Hamon.
7. In some Bibles, this book is called *Song of Solomon*; in others, it is *Song of Songs*. *Song of Songs* is the Hebrew title of the book; in addition, the writer calls it that in verse one of chapter one. Some title the book with a nod to **Solomon**, for many scholars have concluded that Israel's third monarch wrote it.
8. The book is also called *Canticles*, its title in the Latin Vulgate.
9. If you ever run out of **compliments** for the girl of your dreams, turn to Song of Songs 7 and then refer to her nose as being "like the tower of Lebanon" and see how that turns out.
10. Nobody knows where **Shulem** was located. Some believe it is synonymous with Shunem. That would make the Shulammite woman (the object of the writer's affection) a resident of a village north of the Jezreel Valley and south of Mount Gilboa. Another theory is that she was the daughter of a Pharaoh. No matter where she was from, Solomon was quite taken with her.

```
S P C M H F Q P W D Y M X U N
G I Y Q Q A H T A C L P V B Y
V H G R W U R E N O M O L O S
T S A H Q X L T P G A Q J C X
B N X Y J I I Z F O M N K O D
M O B I G Z K Q A A E R N M E
O I K X P O U H U T O T C P N
U T G A Z E L L E S P G J L I
N A U I Y H P A R G O E G I W
T L J I E Y U L C P G M H M Z
C E W G T L H C D L S Z W E T
A R M B O P Q A U O O N Y N G
R W Q V V A T N Z L V W T T S
M U E T Z L N T K H M E D S H
E K Y P A H C I V T X A S I U
L E O L G F V C M Z C Q Q M L
G T A A K F G L B A M B P G E
T C A N S V Z E E G L W U X M
R H X T O K Z S Z F T S P Q F
U N R A T H E W U U S K M A H
```

Answer key on page 88

Song of Songs

1 Solomon's Song of Songs.

She

²Let him kiss me with the kisses of his mouth —
 for your love is more delightful than wine.
³Pleasing is the fragrance of your perfumes;
 your name is like perfume poured out.
 No wonder the young women love you!
⁴Take me away with you — let us hurry!
 Let the king bring me into his chambers.

Friends

We rejoice and delight in you;
 we will praise your love more than wine.

She

How right they are to adore you!

⁵Dark am I, yet lovely,
 daughters of Jerusalem,
 dark like the tents of Kedar,
 like the tent curtains of Solomon.
⁶Do not stare at me because I am dark,
 because I am darkened by the sun.
 My mother's sons were angry with me
 and made me take care of the vineyards;
 my own vineyard I had to neglect.
⁷Tell me, you whom I love,
 where you graze your flock
 and where you rest your sheep at midday.
 Why should I be like a veiled woman
 beside the flocks of your friends?

Friends

⁸If you do not know, most beautiful of women,
 follow the tracks of the sheep
 and graze your young goats
 by the tents of the shepherds.

He

⁹I liken you, my darling, to a mare
 among Pharaoh's chariot horses.
¹⁰Your cheeks are beautiful with earrings,
 your neck with strings of jewels.
¹¹We will make you earrings of gold,
 studded with silver.

She

¹²While the king was at his table,
 my perfume spread its fragrance.
¹³My beloved is to me a sachet of myrrh
 resting between my breasts.
¹⁴My beloved is to me a cluster of henna blossoms
 from the vineyards of En Gedi.

He

¹⁵How beautiful you are, my darling!
 Oh, how beautiful!
 Your eyes are doves.

Song of Songs is also known as "The Song of Solomon" or "Canticles."

```
F B O X M L S R U P R K C Q X I P S V
Y I A R N O T C H E E K S H M Y R R H
Q R Y D T V A G T B A Q Z B K E A S N
B L R M D E O R S R E B M A H C J S R
A N U U G L G I N K A K V I Y Z E R F
Q D U F H Y B E S T C C G U D X R U A
Y F X V T E R B M E B H K F V L S A V
E W R I T H G O N A B A F S T J E L P
A C R N B G G G M I N R T E B L Y J H
R A J E A Z M I N L N I U S B F E N M
R C A Y B N M Q L J P O E A I N W D X
I E T A N J N Z H E S T T V S T A H F
N M X R M R M E J D D S E M U F R E P
G R R D B P F X H N U C L J W Z G Z Z
S R C S G N W W C R I L Z T N Y J K K
```

1. The bride says to her groom, "Your love is more _ _ _ _ _ _ _ _ _ _ than wine." (1:2)
2. Pleasing is the fragrance of his _ _ _ _ _ _ _ _. (1:3)
3. His _ _ _ _ _ is like perfume poured out. (1:3)
4. She says to him, "Take me away with you—let us _ _ _ _ _!" (1:4)
5. "Let the king bring me into his _ _ _ _ _ _ _ _." (1:4)
6. She says, "Dark am I, yet _ _ _ _ _ _ _." (1:5)
7. Her mother's sons made her take care of the _ _ _ _ _ _ _ _ _ _. (1:6)
8. The Friends say to follow the _ _ _ _ _ _ _ of the sheep. (1:8)
9. They say to graze young _ _ _ _ _ _ by the tents of the shepherds. (1:8)
10. The bride is like a mare among Pharaoh's _ _ _ _ _ _ _ _ horses. (1:9)
11. Her _ _ _ _ _ _ _ are beautiful with earrings. (1:10)
12. Her _ _ _ _ is adorned with strings of jewels. (1:10)
13. They will make her _ _ _ _ _ _ _ _ _ of gold. (1:11)
14. While the king was at his _ _ _ _ _ _, the bride's perfume spread its fragrance. (1:12)
15. Her beloved is to her a sachet of _ _ _ _ _ _. (1:13)
16. He is to her a cluster of _ _ _ _ _ _ blossoms. (1:14)
17. The groom says the bride is beautiful, and her _ _ _ _ _ are doves. (1:15)

Answer key on page 89

She

¹⁶ How handsome you are, my beloved!
    Oh, how charming!
And our bed is verdant.

He

¹⁷ The beams of our house are cedars;
    our rafters are firs.

She

2 I am a rose of Sharon,
    a lily of the valleys.

He

² Like a lily among thorns
    is my darling among the young women.

She

³ Like an apple tree among the trees of the forest
    is my beloved among the young men.
I delight to sit in his shade,
    and his fruit is sweet to my taste.
⁴ Let him lead me to the banquet hall,
    and let his banner over me be love.
⁵ Strengthen me with raisins,
    refresh me with apples,
    for I am faint with love.
⁶ His left arm is under my head,
    and his right arm embraces me.
⁷ Daughters of Jerusalem, I charge you
    by the gazelles and by the does of the field:
Do not arouse or awaken love
    until it so desires.

⁸ Listen! My beloved!
    Look! Here he comes,
leaping across the mountains,
    bounding over the hills.
⁹ My beloved is like a gazelle or a young stag.
Look! There he stands behind our wall,
    gazing through the windows,
    peering through the lattice.
¹⁰ My beloved spoke and said to me,
    "Arise, my darling,
    my beautiful one, come with me.
¹¹ See! The winter is past;
    the rains are over and gone.
¹² Flowers appear on the earth;
    the season of singing has come,
the cooing of doves
    is heard in our land.
¹³ The fig tree forms its early fruit;
    the blossoming vines spread their fragrance.
Arise, come, my darling;
    my beautiful one, come with me."

He

¹⁴ My dove in the clefts of the rock,
    in the hiding places on the mountainside,
show me your face,
    let me hear your voice;
for your voice is sweet,
    and your face is lovely.
¹⁵ Catch for us the foxes,
    the little foxes
that ruin the vineyards,
    our vineyards that are in bloom.

She

¹⁶ My beloved is mine and I am his;
    he browses among the lilies.
¹⁷ Until the day breaks
    and the shadows flee,
turn, my beloved,
    and be like a gazelle
or like a young stag
    on the rugged hills.

This poem is primarily told from the bride's perspective.

```
A H Q W S Q V Z I N A K F Y L I L T Z
J T R N S R A D E C D N A E R B V W D
J O S E S H A R O N L L N G U Q I I B
Y C X G L K J D R O X B A U X Z N N I
T O J H Z Q L P B G A Z G K D N E T V
F N C J Z D O V E S E E Z K F M S E B
L A A M N C U F F L Z V J A Y C Y R U
O H P F K H V E L N R E N N A B M O Z
W S R P N S O E G K U E S N A B A I R
E Y U U L I W L R Z S H V H Q Q H V E
R L G U E E K R D D P G Y K L I G N O
S U G U X T E U Q N A B I F Z B I G R
O G E A T N P M R H B N K M I M D U C
C R D V W Q Z A N T E T T M E G Q W X
V T C O C B T B U Q O Y U O Z J X S H
```

1. Their bed is _ _ _ _ _ _ _ _. (1:16)
2. The beams of their house are _ _ _ _ _ _. (1:17)
3. The bride is a rose of _ _ _ _ _ _. (2:1)
4. She is a _ _ _ _ of the valleys. (2:1)
5. The groom is like an _ _ _ _ _ _ tree among the trees of the forest. (2:3)
6. Let him lead his bride to the _ _ _ _ _ _ _ _ hall. (2:4)
7. Let his _ _ _ _ _ _ _ over her be love. (2:4)
8. The bride's beloved is like a _ _ _ _ _ _ _ _ or a young stag. (2:9)
9. The _ _ _ _ _ _ is past; the rains are over and gone. (2:11)
10. _ _ _ _ _ _ _ appear on the earth. (2:12)
11. The cooing of _ _ _ _ _ is heard in their land. (2:12)
12. The _ _ _ tree forms its early fruit. (2:13)
13. The blossoming _ _ _ _ _ spread their fragrance. (2:13)
14. The little _ _ _ _ _ ruin the vineyards. (2:15)
15. The bride declares, "My beloved is _ _ _ _ _ and I am his." (2:16)
16. She tells him, "Be like a gazelle on the _ _ _ _ _ _ _ hills." (2:17)

Answer key on page 89

65

3 ¹All night long on my bed
I looked for the one my heart loves;
I looked for him but did not find him.
²I will get up now and go about the city,
through its streets and squares;
I will search for the one my heart loves.
So I looked for him but did not find him.
³The watchmen found me
as they made their rounds in the city.
"Have you seen the one my heart loves?"
⁴Scarcely had I passed them
when I found the one my heart loves.
I held him and would not let him go
till I had brought him to my mother's house,
to the room of the one who conceived me.
⁵Daughters of Jerusalem, I charge you
by the gazelles and by the does of the field:
Do not arouse or awaken love
until it so desires.

⁶Who is this coming up from the wilderness
like a column of smoke,
perfumed with myrrh and incense
made from all the spices of the merchant?
⁷Look! It is Solomon's carriage,
escorted by sixty warriors,
the noblest of Israel,
⁸all of them wearing the sword,
all experienced in battle,
each with his sword at his side,
prepared for the terrors of the night.
⁹King Solomon made for himself the carriage;
he made it of wood from Lebanon.
¹⁰Its posts he made of silver,
its base of gold.
Its seat was upholstered with purple,
its interior inlaid with love.
Daughters of Jerusalem, ¹¹come out,
and look, you daughters of Zion.
Look on King Solomon wearing a crown,
the crown with which his mother crowned him
on the day of his wedding,
the day his heart rejoiced.

He

4 ¹How beautiful you are, my darling!
Oh, how beautiful!
Your eyes behind your veil are doves.
Your hair is like a flock of goats
descending from the hills of Gilead.
²Your teeth are like a flock of sheep just shorn,
coming up from the washing.
Each has its twin;
not one of them is alone.
³Your lips are like a scarlet ribbon;
your mouth is lovely.
Your temples behind your veil
are like the halves of a pomegranate.
⁴Your neck is like the tower of David,
built with courses of stone;
on it hang a thousand shields,
all of them shields of warriors.
⁵Your breasts are like two fawns,
like twin fawns of a gazelle
that browse among the lilies.
⁶Until the day breaks
and the shadows flee,
I will go to the mountain of myrrh
and to the hill of incense.
⁷You are altogether beautiful, my darling;
there is no flaw in you.

The groom praises his bride's features, delighting in her beauty.

```
E V W Q Q C E R N N K F B S F B D Q X
H Q K J D L L T E A E I A R S M O K E
L H V K R E P W X V L C C X D G Y M J
O I S S B E R H L R L R K A H R C N D
S W P R E K U H T J O I F J P Z M J B
P F D S Y L P V P W C P S L F L Q K S
G S I B G D P M N K Y H C W A M X O S
C Z H W J D V M S U R U M A E W G M E
A X A P Q W F Q E B E A U T I F U L N
R W I S C J E L H T Y H S C R N B E R
R F R F L D B M L T N L P H J E E B E
I Y R X W V Z I I U J K R M K W I A D
A Z M Y R R H C G L S J Z E K L I N L
G E S N E C N I V Q O V M N B E D O I
E I Q Z N G D O P X Q F V B J X K N W
```

1. All night long on her __ __ __, the bride looked for the one her heart loves. (3:1)
2. She will go about the __ __ __ __ __, through its streets and squares. (3:2)
3. The __ __ __ __ __ __ __ __ __ found her as they made their rounds. (3:3)
4. She asks, "Who is this coming up from the __ __ __ __ __ __ __ __ __ __ ?" (3:6)
5. He is coming up like a column of __ __ __ __ __ __, perfumed with myrrh and incense. (3:6)
6. It is Solomon's __ __ __ __ __ __ __ __ __ __, escorted by sixty warriors. (3:7)
7. King Solomon made the carriage of wood from __ __ __ __ __ __ __ __. (3:9)
8. Its posts he made of __ __ __ __ __ __ __, its base of gold. (3:10)
9. Its seat was upholstered with __ __ __ __ __ __ __. (3:10)
10. King Solomon is wearing a __ __ __ __ __ __. (3:11)

11. The bride's __ __ __ __ is like a flock of goats descending from Gilead. (4:1)
12. Her __ __ __ __ __ are like a scarlet ribbon. (4:3)
13. Her __ __ __ __ __ __ __ __ __ are like the halves of a pomegranate. (4:3)
14. Her __ __ __ __ __ is like the tower of David, built with stone. (4:4)
15. The groom will go to the mountain of __ __ __ __ __ __. (4:6)
16. He will go to the hill of __ __ __ __ __ __ __ __. (4:6)
17. He says to his bride, "You are altogether __ __ __ __ __ __ __ __ __ __, my darling." (4:7)
18. "There is no __ __ __ __ __ in you." (4:7)

Answer key on page 89

⁸Come with me from Lebanon, my bride,
  come with me from Lebanon.
 Descend from the crest of Amana,
  from the top of Senir, the summit of Hermon,
 from the lions' dens
  and the mountain haunts of leopards.
⁹You have stolen my heart, my sister, my bride;
 you have stolen my heart
  with one glance of your eyes,
  with one jewel of your necklace.
¹⁰How delightful is your love, my sister, my bride!
  How much more pleasing is your love than wine,
 and the fragrance of your perfume
  more than any spice!
¹¹Your lips drop sweetness as the honeycomb, my bride;
  milk and honey are under your tongue.
 The fragrance of your garments
  is like the fragrance of Lebanon.
¹²You are a garden locked up, my sister, my bride;
  you are a spring enclosed, a sealed fountain.
¹³Your plants are an orchard of pomegranates
  with choice fruits,
  with henna and nard,
¹⁴ nard and saffron,
   calamus and cinnamon,
   with every kind of incense tree,
   with myrrh and aloes
   and all the finest spices.
¹⁵You are a garden fountain,
  a well of flowing water
   streaming down from Lebanon.

She
¹⁶Awake, north wind,
  and come, south wind!
 Blow on my garden,
  that its fragrance may spread everywhere.
 Let my beloved come into his garden
  and taste its choice fruits.

He
5 I have come into my garden, my sister, my bride;
  I have gathered my myrrh with my spice.
 I have eaten my honeycomb and my honey;
  I have drunk my wine and my milk.

Friends
 Eat, friends, and drink;
  drink your fill of love.

She
²I slept but my heart was awake.
  Listen! My beloved is knocking:
 "Open to me, my sister, my darling,
  my dove, my flawless one.
 My head is drenched with dew,
  my hair with the dampness of the night."
³I have taken off my robe—
  must I put it on again?
 I have washed my feet—
  must I soil them again?
⁴My beloved thrust his hand through the latch-opening;
  my heart began to pound for him.
⁵I arose to open for my beloved,
  and my hands dripped with myrrh,
  my fingers with flowing myrrh,
   on the handles of the bolt.

Myrrh was a common ingredient in perfumes and fragrant oils.

```
F M P R P W X W I T L F T S A N P W R
K I L I H B N F J G C I S B B P U R T
V A O T T J P G V R H R J G S G Q K D
Z V V F Q G N S O K E R O F B H A C E
W C E T M I S E T A N A R G E M O P W
U V I D K D C H S J N P A G Q P E M L
K C N C R A Y O E E A F Z P A Z Q Q K
T J O G L S B N O I M O D W T R D M F
Q N U K U D J E L O W U X Z C T D L N
K A C J D F E Y A L K N F Y M W Z E O
H E D M X W I C L Z T T C R K N T J N
N E C K I G P O U N D A M Q E G F I A
N S A N U V B M P X W I E G Z P O S B
C V D R M I D B T U Y N C A M A N A E
P B C S T V O J B D G A R M E N T S L
```

1. The groom says to his beloved, "Come with me from _ _ _ _ _ _ _ _, my bride." (4:8)
2. "Descend from the crest of _ _ _ _ _ _." (4:8)
3. He tells her she has stolen his _ _ _ _ _ _. (4:9)
4. She has stolen it with one jewel of her _ _ _ _ _ _ _ _ _. (4:9)
5. Her _ _ _ _ _ is much more pleasing than wine. (4:10)
6. The fragrance of her _ _ _ _ _ _ _ _ is more pleasing than any spice. (4:10)
7. Her lips drop sweetness as the _ _ _ _ _ _ _ _ _ _ _. (4:11)
8. The fragrance of her _ _ _ _ _ _ _ _ _ _ is like Lebanon. (4:11)
9. She is a _ _ _ _ _ _ _ locked up. (4:12)
10. Her plants are an orchard of _ _ _ _ _ _ _ _ _ _ _ _ _ _ _. (4:13)
11. In the orchard are _ _ _ _ _ _ and nard. (4:13)
12. There are also myrrh and _ _ _ _ _. (4:14)
13. She is a garden _ _ _ _ _ _ _ _ _. (4:15)
14. The bride calls out, "Awake, north _ _ _ _ _!" (4:16)
15. The bride awakens because her beloved is _ _ _ _ _ _ _ _ _. (5:2)
16. His head was drenched with _ _ _. (5:2)
17. Her heart began to _ _ _ _ _ _ for him. (5:4)

Answer key on page 89

69

⁶ I opened for my beloved,
  but my beloved had left; he was gone.
  My heart sank at his departure.
 I looked for him but did not find him.
  I called him but he did not answer.
⁷ The watchmen found me
  as they made their rounds in the city.
 They beat me, they bruised me;
  they took away my cloak,
  those watchmen of the walls!
⁸ Daughters of Jerusalem, I charge you—
  if you find my beloved,
 what will you tell him?
  Tell him I am faint with love.

Friends

⁹ How is your beloved better than others,
  most beautiful of women?
 How is your beloved better than others,
  that you so charge us?

She

¹⁰ My beloved is radiant and ruddy,
  outstanding among ten thousand.
¹¹ His head is purest gold;
  his hair is wavy
  and black as a raven.
¹² His eyes are like doves
  by the water streams,
 washed in milk,
  mounted like jewels.
¹³ His cheeks are like beds of spice
  yielding perfume.
 His lips are like lilies
  dripping with myrrh.
¹⁴ His arms are rods of gold
  set with topaz.
 His body is like polished ivory
  decorated with lapis lazuli.
¹⁵ His legs are pillars of marble
  set on bases of pure gold.
 His appearance is like Lebanon,
  choice as its cedars.
¹⁶ His mouth is sweetness itself;
  he is altogether lovely.
 This is my beloved, this is my friend,
  daughters of Jerusalem.

Friends

6 Where has your beloved gone,
  most beautiful of women?
 Which way did your beloved turn,
  that we may look for him with you?

She

² My beloved has gone down to his garden,
  to the beds of spices,
 to browse in the gardens
  and to gather lilies.
³ I am my beloved's and my beloved is mine;
  he browses among the lilies.

He

⁴ You are as beautiful as Tirzah, my darling,
  as lovely as Jerusalem,
  as majestic as troops with banners.
⁵ Turn your eyes from me;
  they overwhelm me.
 Your hair is like a flock of goats
  descending from Gilead.
⁶ Your teeth are like a flock of sheep
  coming up from the washing.
 Each has its twin,
  not one of them is missing.
⁷ Your temples behind your veil
  are like the halves of a pomegranate.

Solomon used Lebanon's famous cedar trees to build the temple in Jerusalem.

```
W W T A I R G Q P T O V X X C T O E Z
H C T T S R G O L D C W C N W I F H O
W O E L I L I E S W Y I A G S V Y X D
A A E D X M U I Y H I C P S L O V U I
T U T J A O M S E L P M E T A R A P F
C U G Y T R G R Y O L N G S O Y W C V
H J P U R F S P Z S T Y B A J N N S D
M I O F X N E A O E V B D Y S H P M E
E J E R U S A L E M Q C J A C I N T K
N J J H M G P W D T A G Q F C E W N H
E T A Z I Y S A K B K V Z E L B B A H
F Y U A F A I N T F F Q U B K L L I Y
E C E P W O Y H R D X O R Q R X G D G
U L B S T F W H Y U D A P H A I R A X
K V G A R D E N O Q M R H V L M W R K
```

1. The bride opened for her beloved, but her beloved had _ _ _ _. (5:6)
2. The _ _ _ _ _ _ _ _ _ found her as they made their rounds. (5:7)
3. The bride says she is _ _ _ _ _ _ with love. (5:8)
4. Her beloved is _ _ _ _ _ _ _ _ and ruddy. (5:10)
5. His hair is _ _ _ _ _ and black as a raven. (5:11)
6. His _ _ _ _ _ are like doves by the water streams. (5:12)
7. His cheeks are like beds of _ _ _ _ _ _. (5:13)
8. His lips are like _ _ _ _ _ _ _ dripping with myrrh. (5:13)
9. His arms are rods of _ _ _ _ set with topaz. (5:14)
10. His body is like polished _ _ _ _ _ _. (5:14)
11. His legs are pillars of _ _ _ _ _ _ _. (5:15)
12. His appearance is like Lebanon, choice as its _ _ _ _ _ _ _. (5:15)
13. His mouth is _ _ _ _ _ _ _ _ _ _ itself. (5:16)
14. The bride's beloved has gone down to his _ _ _ _ _ _. (6:2)
15. He tells her she is as lovely as _ _ _ _ _ _ _ _ _. (6:4)
16. Her _ _ _ _ is like a flock of goats descending from Gilead. (6:5)
17. Her _ _ _ _ _ _ _ _ are like the halves of a pomegranate. (6:7)

Answer key on page 89

⁸Sixty queens there may be,
 and eighty concubines,
 and virgins beyond number;
⁹but my dove, my perfect one, is unique,
 the only daughter of her mother,
 the favorite of the one who bore her.
 The young women saw her and called her blessed;
 the queens and concubines praised her.

Friends

¹⁰Who is this that appears like the dawn,
 fair as the moon, bright as the sun,
 majestic as the stars in procession?

He

¹¹I went down to the grove of nut trees
 to look at the new growth in the valley,
 to see if the vines had budded
 or the pomegranates were in bloom.
¹²Before I realized it,
 my desire set me among the royal chariots of my people.

Friends

¹³Come back, come back,
 O Shulammite;
 come back, come back, that we may gaze on you!

He

Why would you gaze on the Shulammite
 as on the dance of Mahanaim?

7 How beautiful your sandaled feet,
 O prince's daughter!
 Your graceful legs are like jewels,
 the work of an artist's hands.
²Your navel is a rounded goblet
 that never lacks blended wine.
 Your waist is a mound of wheat
 encircled by lilies.
³Your breasts are like two fawns,
 like twin fawns of a gazelle.
⁴Your neck is like an ivory tower.
 Your eyes are the pools of Heshbon
 by the gate of Bath Rabbim.
 Your nose is like the tower of Lebanon
 looking toward Damascus.
⁵Your head crowns you like Mount Carmel.
 Your hair is like royal tapestry;
 the king is held captive by its tresses.
⁶How beautiful you are and how pleasing,
 my love, with your delights!
⁷Your stature is like that of the palm,
 and your breasts like clusters of fruit.
⁸I said, "I will climb the palm tree;
 I will take hold of its fruit."
 May your breasts be like clusters of grapes on the vine,
 the fragrance of your breath like apples,
⁹ and your mouth like the best wine.

She

May the wine go straight to my beloved,
 flowing gently over lips and teeth.
¹⁰I belong to my beloved,
 and his desire is for me.
¹¹Come, my beloved, let us go to the countryside,
 let us spend the night in the villages.
¹²Let us go early to the vineyards
 to see if the vines have budded,
 if their blossoms have opened,
 and if the pomegranates are in bloom—
 there I will give you my love.

Pomegranates in the Bible often symbolize abundance, prosperity, and fertility.

```
N D A W N K E T E O Q S A N K G I U S
T E U I G M L E V F G T W K C E H R E
R I Q N T C P I U E V O R G R R U H L
T O W E R W N S D I S J X I V A K G P
D W F V N E H E N O H E S H B O N W P
V T T L Y B S E U H F E O M L N S N A
P D Z A I S P G A C D T W E Z H F J N
O E R N E T R N C T L U M U G L X A U
H D R L L T A P E S T R Y R Z Y V M D
S Y B Y E F I S E T A N A R G E M O P
G I F P G G S W Z C U F G P L V O C J
K E Q G S H E S H U L A M M I T E L P
H S V X E T D I R E Y W H W V T L A Z
N I E O K J E J G H A N T S J U L N R
H F W V D Y R G U J B S V M Q M L E R
```

1. The groom declares, "My _ _ _ _ _, my perfect one, is unique." (6:9)
2. The young women saw her and called her _ _ _ _ _ _ _. (6:9)
3. The queens and concubines _ _ _ _ _ _ _ _ her. (6:9)
4. She appears like the _ _ _ _, fair as the moon, bright as the sun. (6:10)
5. The groom went down to the _ _ _ _ _ _ of nut trees. (6:11)
6. The friends gaze on the _ _ _ _ _ _ _ _ _ _ _ as on the dance of Mahanaim. (6:13)
7. Her graceful _ _ _ _ are like jewels. (7:1)
8. Her _ _ _ _ _ is a rounded goblet that never lacks blended wine. (7:2)
9. Her waist is a mound of _ _ _ _ _ _ encircled by lilies. (7:2)
10. Her breasts are like two _ _ _ _ _. (7:3)
11. Her nose is like the _ _ _ _ _ of Lebanon looking toward Damascus. (7:4)
12. Her head crowns her like Mount _ _ _ _ _ _. (7:5)
13. Her hair is like royal _ _ _ _ _ _ _ _ _. (7:5)
14. Her stature is like that of the _ _ _ _ _. (7:7)
15. The fragrance of her breath is like _ _ _ _ _ _. (7:8)
16. Her mouth is like the best _ _ _ _ _. (7:9)
17. She says, "I belong to my beloved, and his _ _ _ _ _ _ is for me." (7:10)
18. They will go early to the _ _ _ _ _ _ _ _ _ _ to see if the vines have budded. (7:12)
19. If the _ _ _ _ _ _ _ _ _ _ _ _ _ are in bloom, there she will give him her love. (7:12)

Answer key on page 89

73

¹³ The mandrakes send out their fragrance,
   and at our door is every delicacy,
both new and old,
   that I have stored up for you, my beloved.

8

If only you were to me like a brother,
   who was nursed at my mother's breasts!
Then, if I found you outside,
   I would kiss you,
   and no one would despise me.
² I would lead you
   and bring you to my mother's house—
   she who has taught me.
I would give you spiced wine to drink,
   the nectar of my pomegranates.
³ His left arm is under my head
   and his right arm embraces me.
⁴ Daughters of Jerusalem, I charge you:
   Do not arouse or awaken love
   until it so desires.

Friends

⁵ Who is this coming up from the wilderness
   leaning on her beloved?

She

Under the apple tree I roused you;
   there your mother conceived you,
   there she who was in labor gave you birth.
⁶ Place me like a seal over your heart,
   like a seal on your arm;
for love is as strong as death,
   its jealousy unyielding as the grave.
It burns like blazing fire,
   like a mighty flame.
⁷ Many waters cannot quench love;
   rivers cannot sweep it away.
If one were to give
   all the wealth of one's house for love,
   it would be utterly scorned.

Friends

⁸ We have a little sister,
   and her breasts are not yet grown.
What shall we do for our sister
   on the day she is spoken for?
⁹ If she is a wall,
   we will build towers of silver on her.
If she is a door,
   we will enclose her with panels of cedar.

She

¹⁰ I am a wall,
   and my breasts are like towers.
Thus I have become in his eyes
   like one bringing contentment.
¹¹ Solomon had a vineyard in Baal Hamon;
   he let out his vineyard to tenants.
Each was to bring for its fruit
   a thousand shekels of silver.
¹² But my own vineyard is mine to give;
   the thousand shekels are for you, Solomon,
   and two hundred are for those who tend its fruit.

He

¹³ You who dwell in the gardens
   with friends in attendance,
   let me hear your voice!

She

¹⁴ Come away, my beloved,
   and be like a gazelle
or like a young stag
   on the spice-laden mountains.

The last chapter of this book emphasizes commitment and unending love.

```
J P O X S Q V S W I L S C E I W K G E
G W Z S W E E P A A W U N U J W G Y L
H P B H E N Q Q E G Y X I A A T A N T
S D Z E M W K S O A F J K G U R Z H P
S M B K B Y A X Y R O C S T R I E V U
E V G E R D P G Q D C H T X Z A L L R
N I F L A T P S Z E B F N M D M L V U
R W E S C X L M A N D R A K E S E I O
E H X C E T E G W S I T N K G M N N E
D E J G S D E V A O U M E X T G P E W
L F D N P H J A Y N A W T Q V M Y Y A
I X S O G O P V H H A J L H W I F A C
W R M R O E F W R L S J G K I Q I R T
J H C T C R N O L X O G Y N V N R D S
E H X S W A T E R S G B E L O V E D F
```

1. The _____ send out their fragrance. (7:13)
2. The groom's left arm is under his bride's _____. (8:3)
3. His right arm _____ her. (8:3)
4. The bride comes up from the _____ leaning on her beloved. (8:5)
5. She roused her beloved under the _____ tree. (8:5)
6. She tells him, "Place me like a _____ over your heart." (8:6)
7. For love is as _____ as death. (8:6)
8. It burns like blazing _____. (8:6)
9. Many _____ cannot quench love. (8:7)
10. Rivers cannot _____ it away. (8:7)
11. If their little sister is a _____, the Friends will build towers of silver on her. (8:9)
12. If she is a ____, they will enclose her with panels of cedar. (8:9)
13. Solomon let out his vineyard to _____. (8:11)
14. Each was to bring a thousand _____ of silver. (8:11)
15. The bride's own _____ is hers to give. (8:12)
16. She dwells in the _____. (8:13)
17. She calls to the groom, "Come away, my _____." (8:14)
18. She tells him to be like a _____ or a young stag on the spice-laden mountains. (8:14)

Answer key on page 90

Highlights from Song of Songs

The next word search covers the full book of Song of Songs, highlighting some key words and themes from throughout the book.

- APPLES
- BEAUTIFUL
- BELOVED
- BLOSSOMS
- BRIDE
- DARLING
- DELIGHT
- DOVE
- EYES
- FAINT
- FOUNTAIN
- FRAGRANCE
- FRUIT
- GARDEN
- GAZELLE
- GOLD
- HEART
- HONEYCOMB
- JEWELS
- KISS
- LEBANON
- LILIES
- LOVELY
- MYRRH
- PERFUME
- POMEGRANATES
- SEAL
- SHULAMMITE
- TOWER
- VINEYARD

```
L T O E N Z R H B Q W F C P Z D I J D
B Y I H I O E A F U C L C L U G D H M
V N B D A A R W R J L A G E S C R I U
D Y M X R P G W U K M I P B L L A U X
K O O T W U P Q I I H B V A Q X Y R A
W C C O M M C L T B E A V N M B E P C
B L Y B E L O V E D N D M O S W N X Q
L Z E S S I K A O S D L B N O D I P S
K M N Q M A U C F R W G W T H O V S N
B G O X Y T T T A L O V E L Y V S E K
H L H P I D L O G M H L G F D E C I R
S C O F E X Z A O W W U G M A Z B L B
B R U S G A Z E L L E R M F M I S I X
V L T P S E T H M W H H F G C P N L M
S H H R M O C J F S H U L A M M I T E
E M U P G C M T H G I L E D W U E B G
H Q K N I U O S F Y K Z E F Q Y G T N
M M H X S T I C F E S J I M E X N E I
D N X Z H G S H J E W E L S A P I M L
Z S E T A N A R G E M O P T M O A U R
G A W R K W X L S L F M Q Z T K T F A
V D D U O V F B Z I Y C S V K L N R D
O E O K G F R A G R A N C E L K U E D
N S W Z A G F D R G N T B O A Y O P Y
T N U M U S B H G E D I R B I L F E Z
```

Answer key on page 90

77

Song of Songs

ACROSS

5. Like shorn sheep coming up from the washing. (4:2)
7. Like goats descending from Gilead. (4:1)
10. Her temples are like this fruit. (4:3)
11. Aromatic ingredients. (4:14)
12. Sweet to her taste from his tree. (2:3)
17. Symbol of love set upon his heart and arm. (8:6)
18. Features like doves. (1:15)
21. How the groom describes his bride. (1:15)
23. The bride's possession, which is hers to give. (8:12)
25. His body is like this polished material. (5:14)
26. The bride's name for her groom. (2:16)
28. A fragrant spice used in perfume. (3:6)
31. Like David's tower with hanging shields. (4:4)
33. His name is like this poured out. (1:3)
35. Plant he resembles among young men. (2:3)
36. Like twin fawns of a gazelle. (4:5)
37. The poem's opening action. (1:2)

DOWN

1. His legs are like pillars of this material. (5:15)
2. A locked up place, like an enclosed fountain. (4:12)
3. Her graceful legs are like these. (7:1)
4. Cannot quench love. (8:7)
6. Sweet sound he longs to hear. (2:14)
8. Cold season that is past. (2:11)
9. Flowers among which he browses. (2:16)
10. Her stature is like this tall tree. (7:7)
13. Her hair is like this royal material. (7:5)
14. She invites her beloved to be like this animal. (8:14)
15. Sweet substance under her tongue. (4:11)
16. Country the bride is invited to come from. (4:8)
19. His hair is as black as this bird. (5:11)
20. Love is more delightful than this drink. (1:2)
21. The one marrying the groom. (4:8)
22. Spread by the wind from the bride's garden. (4:16)
24. The groom's name for his bride. (6:9)
27. The bride is faint with this. (5:8)
28. He comes leaping across these. (2:8)
29. Though she slept, this remained awake. (5:2)
30. His head is like this precious metal. (5:11)
32. Solomon's wedding gift from his mother. (3:11)
34. Love burns like this. (8:6)

Answer key on page 90

79

ANSWER KEY

PAGE 7

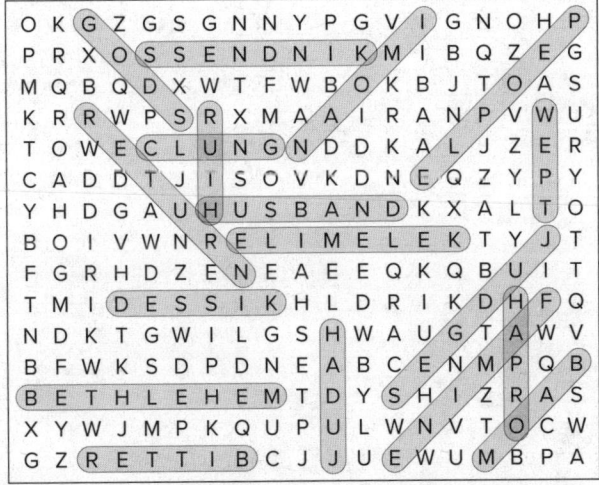

PAGE 9

PAGE 11

PAGE 13

PAGE 15

PAGE 17

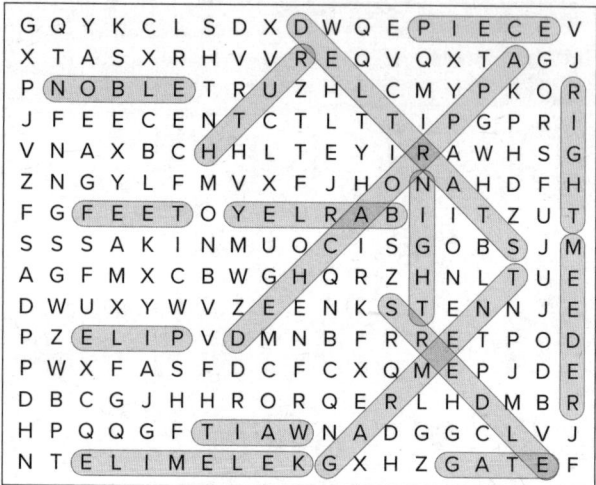

PAGE 19

PAGE 21

PAGE 23

PAGE 27

PAGE 29

PAGE 31

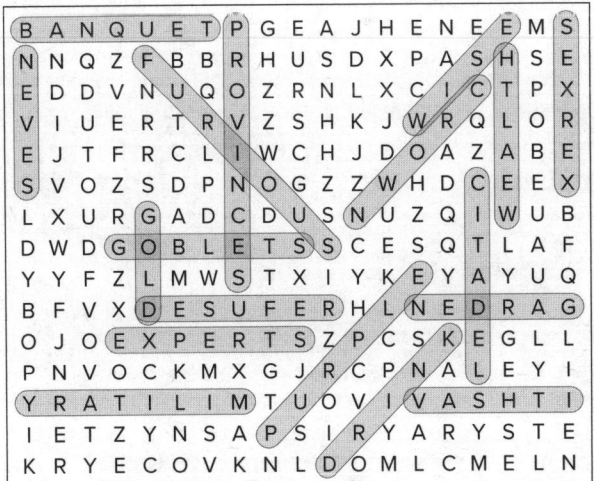

PAGE 33

PAGE 35

PAGE 37

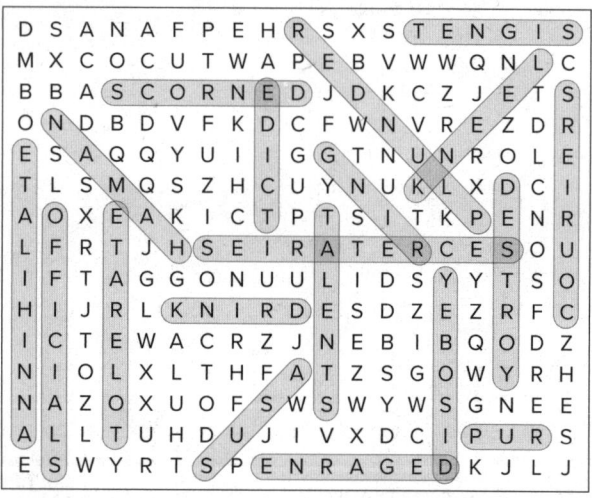

PAGE 39

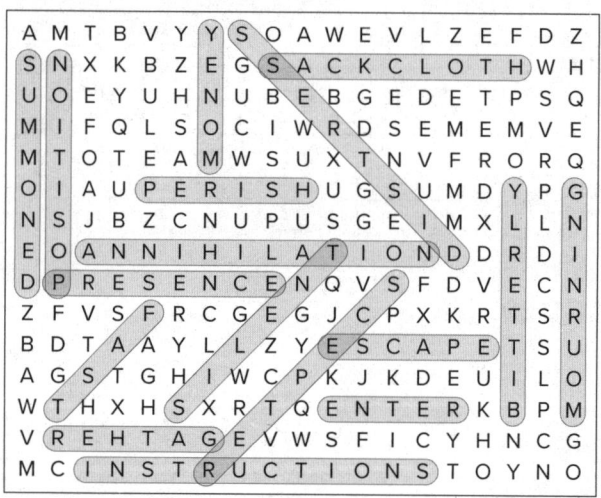

PAGE 41

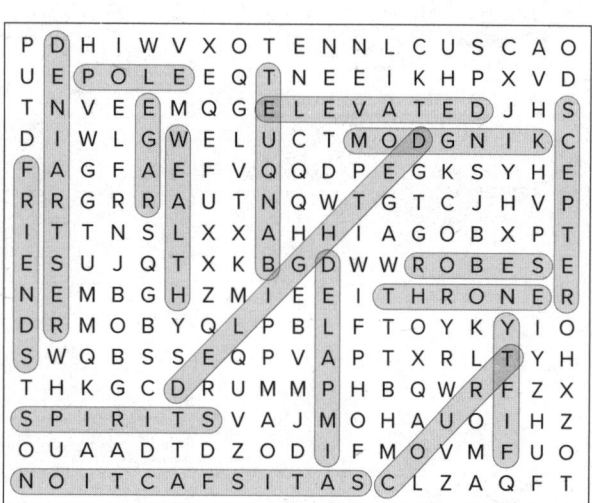

PAGE 43

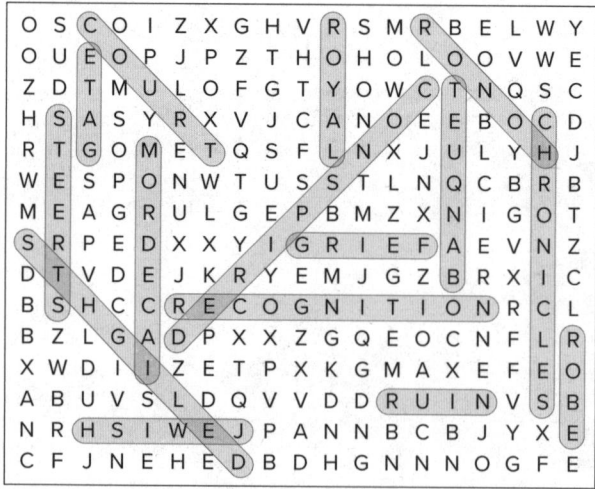

PAGE 45

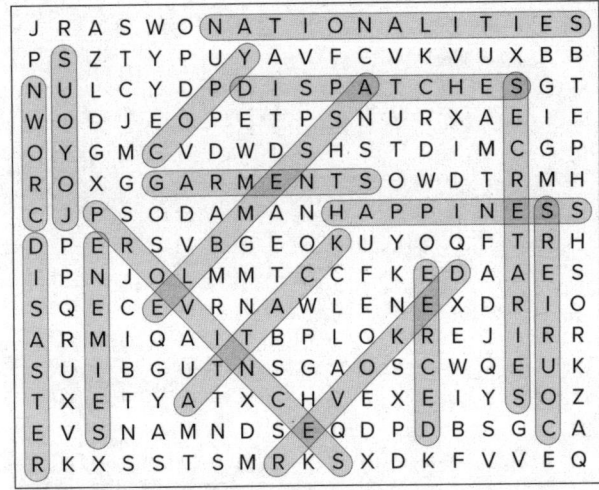

PAGE 47

PAGE 49

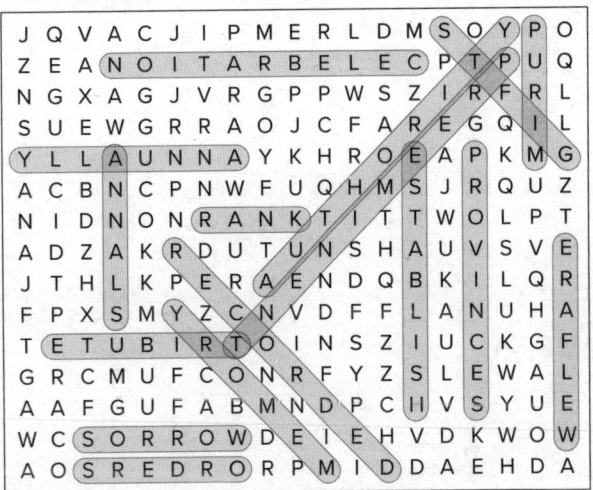

PAGE 51

PAGE 53

PAGE 55

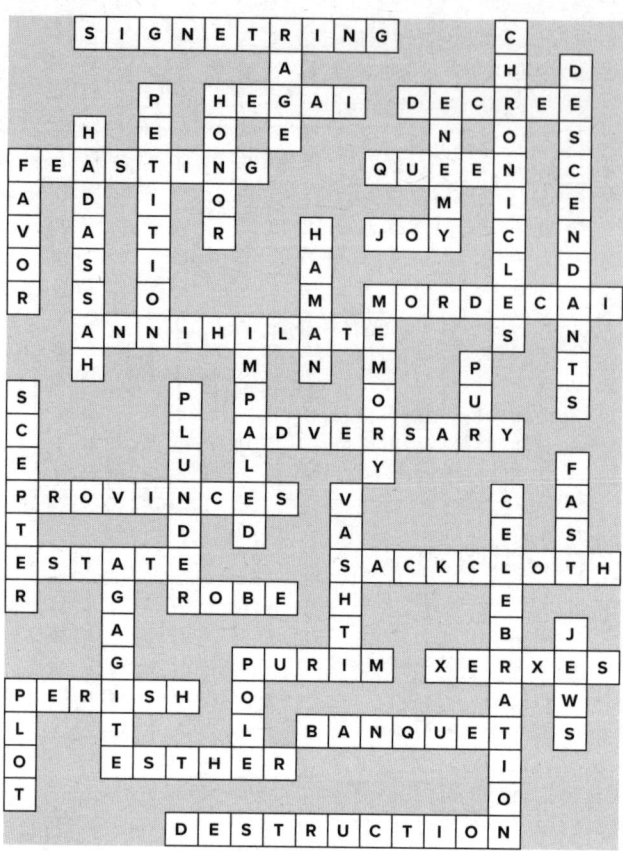

PAGE 59

PAGE 61

PAGE 63

PAGE 65

PAGE 67

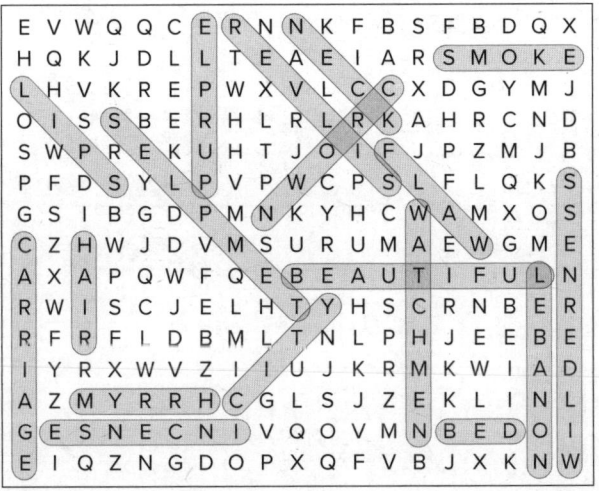

PAGE 69

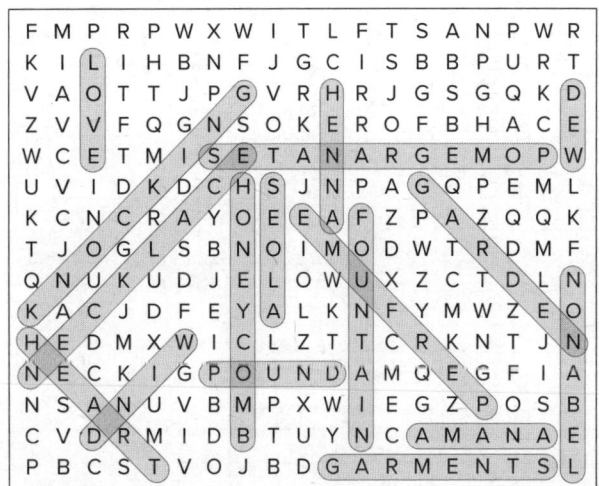

PAGE 71

PAGE 73

PAGE 75

PAGE 77

PAGE 79

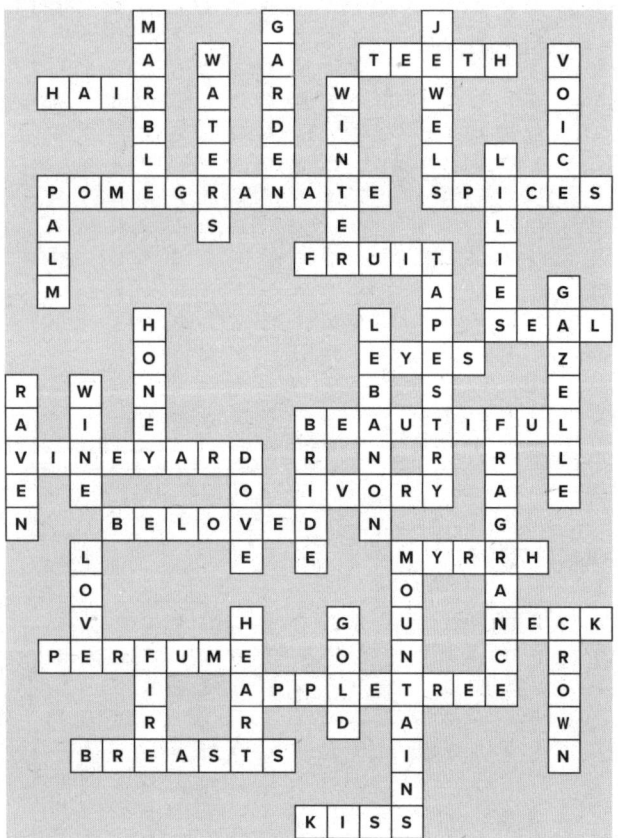

Faith-filled Fun for Every Generation

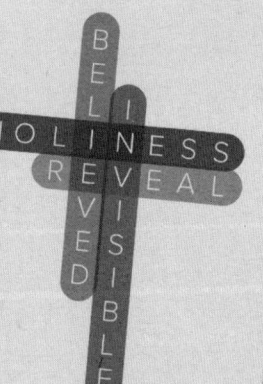

With full NIV Bible text, *Search the Scriptures* word find series provides nourishment for both mind and spirit!

Puzzle Your Way Through the Word

Search the Scriptures
A Word Find Book *from* Our Daily Bread Ministries

Ruth
Esther
Song of Songs

Available Fall 2025

Search the Scriptures
A Word Find Book *from* Our Daily Bread Ministries

James
1 & 2 Peter
1, 2 & 3 John
Jude

Available Spring 2026

Available at Our Daily Bread Publishing or wherever books are sold.

Spread the Word by Doing One Thing.

- Give a copy of this book as a gift.
- Share the QR code link via your social media.
- Write a review of this book on your blog, favorite bookseller's website, or at ourdailybreadpublishing.org.
- Recommend this book to your church, small group, or book club.

Connect with us.

Our Daily Bread Publishing
PO Box 3566, Grand Rapids, MI 49501, USA
Email: books@odbm.org

Love God. Love Others.
with Our Daily Bread.

Your gift changes lives.

Connect with us.

Our Daily Bread Publishing
PO Box 3566, Grand Rapids, MI 49501, USA
Email: books@odbm.org